MURDER
BY THE SEA

MURDER
BY THE SEA

TRUE CRIME STORIES FROM OUR SINISTER SHORES

**DAVID HOWARD
& ROBIN JAROSSI**

MARDLE

First published in 2022 by Mardle Books
15 Church Road
London, SW13 9HE
www.mardlebooks.com

Text © 2022 Monster Films (Wales) Limited

Paperback ISBN 9781914451645
eBook ISBN 9781914451669

A CIP catalogue record for this book is available from the British Library.

Every reasonable effort has been made to trace copyright-holders of material
reproduced in this book, but if any have been inadvertently overlooked the
publishers would be glad to hear from them.

Page design and typesetting by Danny Lyle

Printed in the UK

10 9 8 7 6 5 4 3 2 1

Cover image: Clive Collier
Maps and inserts: Chris Butters/Mirrorpix

To my mother Valerie, who warned
me of the dangers of the seaside.
David Howard

For Vinnie, my father, who threw
me a lifeline when I was adrift.
Robin Jarossi

Contents

STEPHEN AKINMURELE
Blackpool

MATHEW HARDMAN
Anglesey

JOHN COOPER
Pembrokeshire Coastline

PENNY JOHN AND BARRY ROGERS
Johnston, Pembrokeshire

ROBERT MOCHRIE
Barry

LOUISA MAY MERRIFIELD
Blackpool

MITCHELL QUY
Southport

PAUL LONGWORTH
Southport

MALCOLM GREEN
St Brides

PIERRE LEGRIS
Bournemouth

Introduction

The 10 cases explored in these pages all featured in the documentary series *Murder by the Sea*, which launched on the CBS Reality channel in 2018. Independent production company Monster Films produces the programmes, guided by producer Rik Hall and director David Howard.

In a short time, the series has attracted a growing viewership interested in some of the most extraordinary cases from around Britain's coastal communities. The programme has spoken to relatives of murder victims, vital witnesses, former detectives, forensic experts and criminologists. The accounts told have been revelatory and heartbreaking, and occasionally uplifting. Sometimes, the workings of the justice system have been perplexing, at other times the forensic triumphs have been thrilling. The members of the public who have told their stories here, along with the determined police officers, pathologists and forensic scientists, are inspirational and have compelling tales to tell.

David Howard interviewed them all for the programmes. The time constraints of each episode mean there are always more good insights and detail from interviewees than can be included on-screen. Happily, this omitted material has been included in these pages.

I have welcomed the opportunity to be a contributor to some of the *Murder by the Sea* programmes myself. Going through all the transcripts and films for this book has been an object lesson in how much painstaking work, research and skill goes into each episode.

The seaside has proved a fascinating setting for this true-crime series. We head to the coast for the views, the fresh air, the freedom. We go there to retire, to holiday, for a better quality of life.

And yet, the seaside is a place of contrasts. Sunshine and darkness, laughter and fake bonhomie, good times and tragedy.

RJ

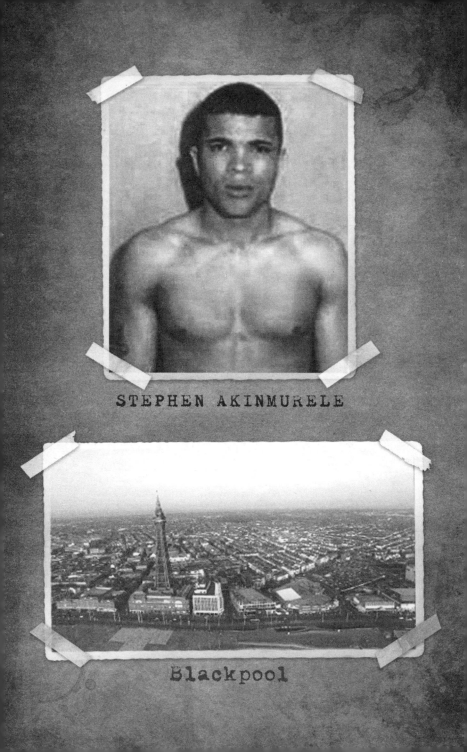

STEPHEN AKINMURELE

Blackpool

1

"He was more concerned about his chips than being arrested on suspicion of murder"

Isle of Man, 1995–1996, and Blackpool, 1998
Victims: Marjorie Ashton, Dorothy Harris,
Jemima Cargill, Joan and Eric Boardman
Murderer: Stephen Akinmurele

Blackpool was a famous leisure resort when Las Vegas was still a broken-down desert fort in the Wild West. Even today it rather cheekily thinks of itself as the entertainment capital of the world. This is despite having fallen on tough times in the latter part of the 20th century. However, there is no doubting its heritage as *the* resort where British working people could forget their cares and have a boisterous time.

By the end of the 19th century Blackpool was a byword for pleasure and amusements. Its landmarks – the Winter Gardens, the Grand Theatre, its three piers, thrilling rides at the Pleasure Beach (visited by the folks from Disney when they were planning Disneyland), Blackpool Tower, and miles of fine sandy beaches – made it Britain's grandest resort. Sea-front trams have run along the prom for more than 135 years, and several miles of illuminations add a sprinkle of magic in the months leading up to Christmas and New Year. To accommodate the influx of holidaymakers, streets of lodgings and boarding houses sprang up around Blackpool's main train stations, in addition to the grand hotels that were built in the late 19th and early 20th centuries.

When it comes to its status as a showbiz Mecca, Blackpool could certainly once have given Vegas a run for its money. Frank Sinatra, Judy Garland, Julie Andrews, Nat King Cole, Elton John and Johnny Cash have taken a bow there, and many more besides. One concert bill from the Opera House in August 1964 that has passed into local legend had The Beatles, The Kinks and The High Numbers (soon to be renamed The Who) appearing on the same line-up.

It was after the Second World War that Blackpool's glitter began to fade. It experienced high rates of crime, seasonal unemployment, the poverty associated with old age, low wages and poor housing. Headlines about benefits claimants filling its bed and breakfasts, polluted beaches, drunkenness and litter also dented the town's image. By 2004, violent crime, car thefts and stealing from cars were at levels almost 50 per cent higher than the average for Lancashire. Visitor numbers were also declining: by 2008 Blackpool offered 60,000 bed spaces, 40 per cent down on 1987.

The town's fortunes never got so desperate that they might justify the lines sung by Morrissey in 1988's hit 'Everyday Is Like Sunday': "*The coastal town / That they forgot to shut down / Come, Armageddon, come!*" Despite the shifting social and economic realities, Blackpool could still attract investment.

In the 1980s and early 1990s new developments were built, including the £16 million Sandcastle swimming pool, an indoor bowling rink and ten-pin bowling complexes, as well as revamps for the Winter Gardens and the Tower.

Blackpool continues to look to a new future, but even in its heyday there was a shady side to the giddy day trips and sunny escapism. A huge resort with millions of visitors and seasonal workers flooding in each year was always going to attract a minority of disaffected, troubled and anti-social people among the fun-seekers. Like its smaller, sister resorts, Blackpool is literally and metaphorically on the edge, a place where normal rules and accepted behaviours are suspended. Strangers intermingle, dirty weekends are had, people let themselves go.

Some break the law.

"People who are likely to commit crimes are attracted to Blackpool," local councillor Tony Williams said bluntly in 2021. "People come from elsewhere in the country because they want to escape and see Blackpool as an attractive place."

Few of the crimes to occur in Blackpool, however, have been as disturbing as one uncovered in 1998. It was then that a woman stumbled on a particularly distressing murder scene, which shook the residents of Blackpool and made further unwanted headlines for the town.

The resulting investigation exposed a terrible series of homicides that had started on the Isle of Man and continued in Blackpool. The bustling resort had become a haven for a young murderer, who blended in with local people while he targeted further victims, a pattern followed by many serial killers. Blackpool had been the scene of notorious murders in the past. Housekeeper Louisa May Merrifield became known as the Blackpool Poisoner after she murdered her employer in 1953 (see Chapter 10). Then, in 1989, former cabbie Michael Downs was convicted of two particularly callous killings. What these murders had in common with the 1998 case was that the victims all came from a demographic that featured strongly in Blackpool and many seaside towns: people living in retirement.

On Friday, 30 October 1998, Marelyn Manning was going to spend the morning with her mother, Joan Boardman. This was a longstanding routine for the pair. Marelyn would take her mum to the shops and get a coffee three or four times a week. She would drop by in a taxi, collect mum, who was always waiting on the doorstep of her home on quiet Seafield Road, North Shore, and they would be driven into town.

"When I got there on that Friday morning, she wasn't there," Marelyn recalled. "It didn't enter my mind there was a problem. I just thought, *Oh, she's just held up for a minute. She's talking to Dad or she'll be on the phone.*"

Joan still failed to appear after several minutes, so Marelyn got out of the cab and rang the doorbell. When she got no response, she used her door key to let herself into her parents' house.

Remembering this distressing moment, Marelyn, who speaks in a measured, calm manner, said, "I walked into the house,

MARELYN MANNING, DAUGHTER OF JOAN AND ERIC BOARDMAN

and it was just like a stage had been set – it was a really strange sensation. Dad was on the floor. I couldn't see his face at first because there was a little wardrobe that we used to keep the winter clothing in on top of him. But I recognised his footwear and the bottom of his jeans. So I just went up to him saying, 'Dad, are you all right, are you all right?' And I tried to move the wardrobe. It's a very light wardrobe and I've moved it since, but I couldn't. I think it was just panic.

"I thought, *Mum will be going frantic. Where is she? Why isn't she in the hall?*"

Marelyn went to look in the spare room off the hallway. The door was blocked. She said, "I kept pushing at it just to get my head around, and there was no Mum, until I looked down to see what was blocking the door. And it was just like a pile of washing. And the top thing was a blue sheet, so I picked the blue sheet up, and I just saw an arm sticking out and recognised Mum's cardigan. I moved the sheet completely away and found Mum.

"She was on her back, slightly to one side. She just looked so peaceful, as if she'd just gone to sleep. So, I got down on my hands and knees and put my head on her chest to see if she was breathing, or if there was any heartbeat. I couldn't detect anything, but I felt sure she was still alive. I think that was just part of the panic I was going through. I didn't scream, shout. I'm not that kind of person, but I thought, *Right, I've got to get the ambulance here now.*"

Her hands were shaking so much that she kept dialling the wrong numbers. Eventually, having gone outside and enlisted the help of the waiting taxi driver, an ambulance was summoned. When she spoke to the ambulance dispatch woman on the phone, Marelyn followed her instructions on how to check her parents for signs of life. As far as she could tell, her father appeared to be dead, but her mother may still have been alive.

Uniformed officers arrived and asked Marelyn to wait outside the house. The constable asked her if she had had a row with her parents.

"I said, 'No, I've just come to take Mum out and say hello to Dad and found this.'"

A member of the ambulance crew invited Marelyn to sit in the back of the ambulance because she was shaking so much and her legs were "dancing". She turned down their offer to go to the hospital, saying she wanted to stay with her parents.

"The next thing I know," she said, "Detective Inspector Thistlethwaite came up to me and he was so kind, and said, 'Do you feel as though you could give us a statement as to what's happened this morning? It would help us greatly.'"

She was taken to the police station, where she insisted on calling her brother, Anthony. Between them, the siblings visited their parents at least six days a week. She also made a statement, as requested.

The reality of the pain felt by victims of crimes such as this is often glossed over in news reports. But Marelyn spoke movingly of her loss.

"Since I retired, I used to do whatever I could for them, like most people do, whatever help they needed, and my brother

Anthony was the same. All you want to do is look after them and protect them. To think that the last few minutes of their life, they were struggling and knowing they were going to die, that is so hard because, as I say, all I wanted was them to have a happy life and not have any worries. It's difficult to think of them, unfortunately, because that's the last image I have of them. That's what comes into my mind. I have to really push myself to think of the happier photographs of them."

She soon suspected her beloved parents had been attacked. The chaos in their home and the fact that her parents were not aggressive and did not argue brought home the thought that someone else had been in the property.

"I think it was the day after I found them, the police said this was a serious incident," Marelyn said. "And then, within a few hours, they were saying that it was a double murder. It was just so difficult to accept that someone had been in and done that to them. That's all I can say really, it was just very difficult."

Detectives began to piece together what had happened. An intruder had got into the house at around four in the morning, armed with a small cosh made of batteries taped together inside a sock, which was found at the scene. He had waited for Marelyn's parents to get up. He then strangled Joan Boardman, who was 74 years old, and left her at the bottom of the stairs. Her husband, Eric, 76, had come down, found her, and then he had been attacked by the intruder, too.

"There was quite a violent struggle," said Mick Crook, one of the detectives on the case.

Somehow, Eric seems to have revived and taken on his attacker for a second time. He was hit with the homemade cosh. "And then what we think happened was that he stood on Mr Boardman's neck," said Mick Crook. Placing his palm under the bannister, the killer pushed down with his full weight and squeezed the life out of Mr Boardman.

It is possible that the culprit had tried to make it appear that, by placing the small wardrobe over the dead husband, some kind of accident had occurred. The house was searched and forensically examined. Fingerprints were found on the cosh and a palm print – from among hundreds of prints in the house – was taken from the stairs. These matched the prints of a man police already had on their system. It was, detectives would say, because of Mr Boardman's determined resistance that the killer left behind vital fingerprint clues.

The prints belonged to Stephen Akinmurele, aged 20. His address in a flat in Cheltenham Road, North Shore, was found, and within 48 hours of Marelyn having discovered her parents, officers were on their way to arrest him.

They forced entry into his flat and found him in the living room. According to Gary McAnulty, his solicitor, Akinmurele had recently been charged with criminal damage (kicking in the window of an Indian restaurant), so his fingerprints and DNA were on the police system.

Daniel Cassidy was one of the uni-formed arresting officers: "We'd already

MICK CROOK, ONE OF THE DETECTIVES WHO INTERVIEWED STEPHEN AKINMURELE

been shown a photograph of him. Our first job, as is par for the course when we go in, is we will make lots of noise and identify who we are. He was sat on the settee, eating a bag of chips. My colleague asked him who was. He identified himself as Stephen Akinmurele. My colleague formally arrested and cautioned him, and he said to us, could he finish his chips?

"I could not believe what I'd just heard. So I said, 'Do you understand what we've just said to you?' It's clearly important that he understands exactly what we've said. He was more concerned about his chips than being arrested on suspicion of murder."

Akinmurele was not physically or verbally aggressive. While not muscle-bound, he was athletic and the officers knew he was more than capable of resisting arrest.

"We were aware that Mr Boardman had put up a struggle with him," Cassidy said, so their aim was to quickly restrain him. However, the suspect was not resistant. "He didn't appear concerned. He just seemed empty really, when you looked into his eyes, he was just cold, just nothing there, really, devoid of emotion."

Gary McAnulty was the duty solicitor when Akinmurele was taken into custody.

"I spoke to him on the phone and then went down to the police station to meet him," McAnulty said. "It's quite important to build a rapport with the client, especially when it's a serious offence like a murder, because they have to feel comfortable with you."

And his first impression of his new client?

"He was only a young lad, about 20, but quite easy to deal with really, an affable young man. Sometimes they can be very nervous, but he was easy to talk to and take instructions from.

"He was working as a barman in a local sort of fun pub called Rumours, which was popular back then in the town centre, Talbot Square. He would be working night shifts there, until two in the morning. He would normally have to dress up in shorts and a waistcoat-type thing, which was the standard dress for men behind the bar. You had to be quite fit to carry that off, really."

Akinmurele was not forthcoming about the murders during McAnulty's first encounter with him, offering no explanation about what had happened at Seafield Road. The solicitor did not press him at this stage, trying instead to put Akinmurele at ease. However, McAnulty could see the evidence against his client was strong.

Mick Crook was one of the detectives to interview the suspect. Akinmurele was shown a photo of the Boardmans' house and asked if he knew it. He told the detectives that he happened to be passing the house and saw the police activity on the morning the crime was discovered. The officers then asked him if he had ever been inside the property.

"Quite fortunately for us, he said, 'No, I haven't,'" Crook said. "Well, of course, at that stage we knew that he'd been there – there was a palm print under the stairs."

They told Akinmurele of the evidence that put him in the house, the fingerprints on the cosh, the palm print. He admitted nothing at this stage.

The Boardmans' daughter, Marelyn Manning, was assisting police around this time, helping to identify possessions of her parents that had been found in Akinmurele's flat. They were among a number of items he had taken during past burglaries.

"I picked out Mum's pearls and pearl earrings that Stephen had apparently kept as trophies and given to his girlfriend. I was particularly sorry about her pearl necklace, because in August, two months before she died, she'd been given the 10-year all-clear from having had throat cancer. She'd had an operation, chemotherapy, radiotherapy. She'd lost all of her hair, and 10 years later, when we went back for an assessment of the situation, she'd had tests and the doctor said, 'Well, we don't need to see you again, Mrs Boardman, you're all-clear.' And she was so relieved. I went out and bought her the pearl necklace. Considering she didn't like anything tight around her neck, it had surprised me that she did wear it."

Meanwhile, something about Akinmurele changed during his time in custody. Crook explains: "The day progressed, it was now late and his solicitor had just left. My colleague also left, and I was finishing off the paperwork with him [Akinmurele]. I just remember looking at him and saying, 'So where did it all go wrong?' And he said, 'There's more… I'll speak to you tomorrow.'"

The following morning, the custody office called Crook to say Akinmurele wanted to speak to him.

"So I went to see him. He said, 'There's a lady who was in a fire – I strangled her and set fire to her.'"

If Akinmurele was telling the truth, then what had looked like a burglary gone brutally wrong in Seafield Road might actually be part of a far more sinister series of murderous crimes. Police now dug through the files for any fire incidents that might match the details of Akinmurele's claim.

They found one. Earlier, in October 1998, a 75-year-old woman called Jemima Cargill had died in a fire in the guest house she ran on Caunce Street, Blackpool. She had once been Akinmurele's landlady. Because of the fire damage, the death was put down to an accident at the time. Now the detectives quizzed Akinmurele in minute detail about the property and what he had done, down to the layout of the house, where the light switches and doors were, and where the landlady had been sitting when she was discovered. His account was found to be accurate. He had even told officers that he had thrown a key on to the hallway floor as he was leaving, and police found this under ash when they did a search to check his story. This demonstrated that Akinmurele had detailed knowledge of the crime scene.

As one of the officers who had sifted through the ash and debris, Daniel Cassidy got an up-close sense of how devastating this crime had been.

"He has broken into this building," he said, "murdered somebody, and then set fire to that room. It must have been horrendous, she's a frail old lady. To kill anybody is one thing, but to murder a defenceless old lady is horrible."

Of this crime, clinical forensic psychologist Professor Mike Berry said, "I have in the past come across killers who've stayed in the house after they've killed because they want to enjoy the experience. Some of them even end up having food from the house in which they've killed the victim. In this case, he seems to have had food in the house, he seems to have enjoyed being with the dead victim."

Shockingly, Akinmurele was now looking like a triple murderer. But then there were further chilling revelations.

He told detectives he had murdered a fourth woman on the Isle of Man, where he grew up. Again, investigators extracted a detailed account from Akinmurele, who described a place called Ballasalla. When detective Mick Crook flew out to the Isle of Man to check on the story, he was driven by the local CID to Ballasalla. Though the detective had never visited the Isle of Man before, on reaching Glashen Terrace as indicated by Akinmurele, he felt familiar with the location, so well had the killer described it in minute detail, right down to the pub at the end of the street.

"Everything fitted," Crook recalled. "Yes, there had been a body found, and I think that had been written off as an accident as well, but clearly, again, it was one of Mr Akinmurele's deeds."

So Akinmurele would be charged again, this time with the murder of Dorothy Harris, aged 68, a partially blind and deaf pensioner who had died in a house fire in February 1996.

But then detectives uncovered yet another Isle of Man death, which bore many similarities to Dorothy Harris's death. This was the killing of Marjorie Ashton, 72, who was found dead at her Ballasalla home in May 1995. Akinmurele was also charged with her murder in December 1998.

Police in Lancashire and on the Isle of Man now set up a joint incident room to re-examine a number of fatal house fires in Blackpool, along with sudden deaths on the island dating back to 1994.

What was clear was that Lancashire police had a serial killer in custody, one of the youngest and most prolific in British criminal history.

"He was very matter-of-fact, quite cold," said Mick Crook. "The locals of Blackpool were shocked. Yes, we do have murders, a lot of them domestic. But to have a serial killer in their midst, I think, was quite shocking... Akinmurele was calculating, a man with no remorse."

A priority for investigators now was to learn as much as possible about Stephen Akinmurele's background.

He was born on 16 March 1978 in Nigeria. His mother was from the Isle of Man and his father was Nigerian. When his parents separated, his mother took him back to the Isle of Man, where he grew up. He was apparently raised in large part by his strict grandmother.

His solicitor, Gary McAnulty, recalled some details of Akinmurele's background.

"I think his grandmother was still alive on the Isle of Man," he said, "and his mother was still there. I think his father had passed away and he had a number of siblings. But there was nothing that I can recall that particularly meant that he had any sort of grudge against elderly people."

Nevertheless, a hostility towards the old is what he seemed to have, going back quite some time. A couple of years after the murder of her parents, Marelyn Manning travelled to the Isle of Man herself to research Akinmurele's past.

"I spent the day in the library and looked up Stephen Akinmurele," she said. "He'd been in trouble for menacing elderly ladies many years before. I collected quite a lot of newspaper articles about him. He tended to strangle them. I think the Isle of Man police maybe should have looked into it when two ladies had died in questionable circumstances. And he lived fairly close by that."

He was just 17 years old when he murdered Marjorie Ashton. He attacked Dorothy Harris less than a year later. Professor Mike Berry says of this period of Akinmurele's development, "It is unusual, to say the least, to commit two murders at such a young age – as a teenager – and not be caught. The reality is that the police would not necessarily be looking for a teenager. They would be looking for an older person who maybe has broken into the house, a possible burglary that went wrong, and they've killed the victim in the process of the burglary. They're not looking for a young teenager who's going round killing old people."

Where did his dislike of old people come from at such a young age? Prof Berry could only speculate: "It's not clear whether he hated old people or the idea of getting old himself, or whether it was some form of sexual attraction he was disgusted by." Or perhaps he had developed a hostility to his own grandmother, for some reason.

Aged 18, he fled to Blackpool, probably fearful that his crimes on the Isle of Man would be discovered. A lull of around two and a half years in his murderous tendencies followed his move, perhaps explained by the sexual freedom he found in the town. Akinmurele was bisexual and Blackpool's nightlife held many possibilities for a young, good-looking man. By day he had a civil service job at the benefits office, while by night he worked as a barman in Rumours and, according to police, in one of the town's gay bars.

Prof Berry says, "I suspect that on the Isle of Man his sexuality had to be curtailed, but coming to Blackpool he could be quite actively gay without any moral restraint. As I understand it, he was very promiscuous and active in the gay scene. I suspect there was a certain anxiety and guilt about being gay. He came from a culture that is very anti-homosexuality. Nigeria has some of the most restrictive laws about homosexuality in the world. Being in Blackpool, he would be allowed to be much more sexually active, but at the same time I suspect there would have been an element of guilt in his behaviour."

Daniel Cassidy, remembering his time with a uniformed team of Blackpool officers, offers a vivid description of the town centre at this time, which he saw as a punter and as a policeman.

"He [Akinmurele] was probably only four or five years younger than me. So, as a local lad, I used to frequent Rumours nightclub myself. Typical no windows-type place, absolutely jam-packed at weekends and, yeah, it was a pretty fun place to go.

"Every night of the week the town centre would be busy. Certainly, Thursday, Friday and Saturday you couldn't move for people – very different from the town as it is now. It was full of parties, stag parties, things like that, and naturally where you have any concentration of people and introduce alcohol there is going to be trouble. So it was fights, particularly in the town centre, and we used to police the town centre particularly at the weekends."

After working and playing hard in this rather hedonistic scene for more than two years, Akinmurele got the urge to kill again. Why he did so is one of the many unanswered questions about him, along with how he came to choose the victims he did.

With his first Blackpool victim, Jemima Cargill, it is safe to assume he was tempted by proximity – she was his former landlady. Regarding the Boardmans, police told their daughter, Marelyn Manning, that they did not think he knew them. It is likely that he spotted Joan in the neighbourhood. "He lived very close by to Mum and Dad," Marelyn said, "and he may very well have seen my mum, because she used to do shopping for the lady next door. And my mum had arthritis and she walked with a bit of a waddle. They [the police] said Akinmurele told them that he'd seen her and thought she lived alone because it was elderly ladies he went in for, you know, to hurt."

So, Akinmurele had probably been surprised by Eric Boardman when he got into their home.

"Dad didn't go out a lot, he wasn't often seen, where Mum was always walking up and down."

While Akinmurele was forthcoming about his attacks on Jemima Cargill and Dorothy Harris, he also told some lies to mislead the police. He said he had gone to Jemima Cargill's property to carry out a hit on a drug dealer who lived on the top floor. Daniel Cassidy was part of the search team on the premises and he said, "I did search that top flat at the address, and it was full of needles and what you would associate with a drug user as opposed to a drug dealer."

Akinmurele also claimed he had shot a rambler on a hill on the Isle of Man and hidden the gun in a World War II defence bunker. A weapon was found, but no body. Investigators discounted these accounts of a drug-dealer hit and shooting. The first story was likely a smokescreen for his true target, Jemima Cargill. His solicitor, Gary McAnulty, believed he came up with the shooting story to give the Isle of Man police the run-around. He said Akinmurele's dislike of them was obvious because of all the run-ins he had had with them as a youth.

It is hard not to suspect that his claims of a hit and a shooting were also to deflect from his true motivation: to attack old ladies. He was a young man who could not stop himself from murdering old women – and an old man who got in the way. They were no match for him. Was he ashamed of this? He might well have felt that carrying out a hit on a drug dealer would appear more macho than strangling pensioners.

Criminal psychologist Dr Donna Youngs pierces Akinmurele's pretence here. "This is a murderer who has deliberately killed and targeted the most vulnerable victims, the most fragile group of our society," she said. "Stephen Akinmurele doesn't want anybody to believe that he has this avenging agenda against older people. He is trying to convince other people, and himself, that he doesn't have that particular agenda."

Akinmurele was a classic example of a chameleon personality, personable, easy to get on with, but with a depraved compulsion to kill that he kept well hidden from everyone. Gary McAnulty was certainly struck by this dual aspect of his client.

"I was in my late twenties at the time," he said. "I'd been a solicitor for about three years and so he was about 20. I knew the local area, I knew the club that he worked in and some of the people he worked with. He was also a Man United fan, so I could talk to him about football and it was easy to build up a rapport with him."

He also remembers how stunned everyone at Rumours was when Akinmurele was arrested. The killer had got on well with all the bar staff and was known as a bubbly workmate.

Even more than 20 years later, the jarring contradictions in Akinmurele stand out for the solicitor.

"I've dealt with quite a number of murder cases over the years, and this is the only serial killer I've dealt with," McAnulty said. "He was only 20 years of age. Young, good-looking, charming, easy to talk to – in comparison with others that have the potential to be stereotypical murderers, who are violent young men that build their way up to a murder, starting off with assaults, perhaps, and then getting more and more serious. He didn't strike me as anything like that."

While serial killers are numb emotionally and have little remorse for their victims' suffering, that does not mean their crimes do not cause them some inner turmoil.

"The fact that he brought into the equation these extra offences perhaps meant that he wanted to get it off his chest and I think there was an element of guilt there and certainly remorse," said McAnulty. "When it's put to him that these people have got families, I think that sort of hit home to him."

Akinmurele never gave any insight into why he committed his crimes. His solicitor explains what happened next: "The closer he got to trial, he thought that perhaps there was only one way out for him, and he took it."

Akinmurele hanged himself by a ligature made of clothing at Manchester Prison, formerly known as Strangeways, in August 1999. He was 21 years old.

He left a note to his mother.

"I couldn't take any more of feeling like how I do now, always wanting to kill."

At the time he was facing charges for the murders of the Boardmans and Jemima Cargill. The charges against him regarding Marjorie Ashton and Dorothy Harris had been dropped owing to a technicality. Speculation continues to this day about whether police had managed to uncover all of his murders.

During his inquest in October 2000, it was revealed that Akinmurele had made two previous attempts to kill himself. His girlfriend at this time, Amanda Fitch, told the inquest that he had wished the police had never found him and that he did not want to face the trial. He was a month away from being tried at Preston Crown Court when he killed himself – ironically, on the August Bank Holiday weekend, the busiest of the season in Blackpool.

The prison hospital doctor, Andrzej Rozyki, said Akinmurele had told him he would lie in bed thinking about murder. The note, which was found in the killer's pocket, read:

"I know it's not right always thinking like this but it's always on my mind. I can't help the way I feel, what I did was wrong – I know that and I feel for them – but it doesn't mean I won't do it again. I'll keep on having this feeling I'm going mad because I can't take any more of this and that's why I'm saying goodbye."

His solicitor had no inkling he was going to commit suicide.

"He was just so young," McAnulty said. "He had his 21st birthday in Strangeways and took his own life." McAnulty was astonished that somebody so young could commit so many serious offences.

Dr Youngs gives an insight into how Akinmurele could mislead himself as well as those around him.

"The really unsettling thing about Stephen Akinmurele is that he has himself in a victim narrative," she said. "He is the victim in all this. That's his underlying storyline. How do I know that? Because of the way he talks about fearing that he will kill again. This is classic victim perspective on things. He is abdicating responsibility.

"There are no rules, no social norms, nothing makes any sense. They are essentially powerless, that's how they see themselves operating in the world, as powerless, impotent. They are the victim of life, and therefore everything that they do is just something that has been forced upon them, that is necessary for them to survive. They can justify anything because they are always the victim."

Perhaps a surprising element of this tragic case is that, despite the pain of losing her parents, Marelyn Manning did not surrender to understandable feelings of loathing and vengeance.

"I was glad they got him because I wouldn't want this to happen to anybody else," she said. "I can't believe my parents have been killed by a serial killer. It's weird, but I realised that he was ill. I don't think he was just utterly evil. I've never felt hatred."

There was a macabre episode during Akinmurele's time on remand. The detective Mick Crook spoke to him while he was in prison. During their chat, Akinmurele told Crook about pub-quiz night at the jail: "He said, our team are doing really well. We've got a bloke called Shipman on the team."

Harold Shipman was the family doctor and serial killer who killed around 250 of his patients between 1975 and 1998, according to an official inquiry into his crimes, making him Britain's most prolific murderer. He was on remand in Manchester Prison at the same time as Akinmurele. While the coincidence of two serial killers being on the same quiz team may appear to be some kind of grim cosmic joke, there were further parallels between the men. Both hanged themselves and both targeted the same vulnerable group: elderly women (some 80 per cent of Shipman's victims were women in their senior years).

While Akinmurele's crimes were on a smaller scale than Shipman's, there are other factors that help to explain why his capture and the plight of his victims is so little known in comparison to the older man's. Shipman's killings were not only extensive, but also raised troubling questions about the accountability and trust placed in Britain's medical community. The publicity accorded to the disgraced doctor drowned out any coverage devoted to the events in Blackpool. In addition, Shipman's case went to trial, where he faced charges of murdering 15 of his female patients and forging the will of one of them. The trial at Preston Crown Court lasted almost four months and exposed how he had administered lethal doses of the painkiller diamorphine. Akinmurele, meanwhile, never had to answer for or explain his crimes, and a full account of his actions never came out.

It fell to Detective Superintendent Bob Denmark of Lancashire police to sum up Akinmurele after the inquest into his death.

"I've interviewed him personally and regard him as one of the most dangerous men I have ever met. I would always have been concerned about his propensity to kill and the risk he would have posed to other people, whether in custody or not."

He also paid tribute to Eric Boardman.

"Akinmurele left Mr Boardman for dead, but he recovered and no doubt decided to tackle him. I have no doubt that Mr Boardman put up a terrific struggle and acted with the utmost bravery in defence of himself and, as he thought at the time, his wife."

In films, TV dramas, books and podcasts, serial killers are often the star of the show, with their victims unjustifiably cast as bit-part players, a chalk outline. While it is natural that we wonder what drives certain people to commit terrible crimes, sight should not be lost of the grief and feelings of desolation caused by people such as Stephen Akinmurele.

For that reason, the last words here should go to Marelyn Manning. When asked how she would like her parents, Joan and Eric Boardman, to be remembered, she said, "My Mum being very friendly with everybody. And Dad just being Dad. He was history and motorbike mad. I just remember them as a loving couple, who helped each other and worked together and then went into retirement together.

"Both were well thought of. Dad was quiet, stayed in a lot. Mum was a little bit more outgoing, but they got on well. In fact, when Dad used to have a summer job, which was his pleasure boat on Blackpool prom, and a winter job, shrimping and being an electrician, Mum went with him on electrical jobs, and she was the one crawling under the floorboards with the wires because Dad was a bit bulky. She just helped him all she could, and when he went shrimping, she went with him at five or six o'clock in the morning.

"When they went on the pleasure boat, Mum wasn't happy just to be there seeing people on and off. She wanted to know how to sail the boat and so she got a boat licence. She was the first lady in the north-west to have a full boatman's licence – not a provisional, a full licence – and she was very proud of that.

"Dad's family were boat people. He carried on from where his family left off and Mum hadn't had a lot to do with the sea till she married Dad, but then she became interested in it, and as I say, she just helped him all the way along.

"Dad used to have wagons that would get the people and then go out to the pleasure boat and load the people on and off. And they just did a 20-minute sail. And he came across quite a few youngsters on lilos floating out to sea and brought them back in – that happened more than once.

"He served in the Second World War. He was on HMS *Renown* and saw quite a bit of action. He didn't talk about it a lot, but when you questioned him, he would tell you about it. He had two brothers who were also on HMS *Renown*. But then they decided to take at least one of them off, in case anything happened to the boat and their parents wouldn't lose all three sons in one go.

"They were well liked and respected. Dad was a quietly spoken man who had no temper in him at all. Mum was the same. And they were respected locally – Mum was known for putting dog chewies through people's doors who owned dogs, she knew them all, and Dad was keen on looking after stray cats. He spent his retired life looking after stray cats."

On the Wyre Estuary in Blackpool there is a plaque commemorating Eric's courage in defending Joan and himself on that October morning in 1998. Joan and Eric were married for 27 years.

PAUL LONGWORTH

Southport

2

"This wasn't a straightforward suicide.
There might well have been a struggle"

Southport, 1997
Victim: Tina Longworth
Murderer: Paul Longworth

On the night of 8 January 1997, Paul Longworth returned to his Peel Street home in Southport to a harrowing scene. In the hallway he found his wife, Tina, aged 29, in her nightie and dressing gown, hanging by the neck from a rope tied to a banister spindle of the floor above.

Upstairs the couple's children, Abby, aged seven, and Matthew, five, were asleep. Longworth cut down his wife and called 999 in a distressed state. He told the ambulance control room operator, "I left her this evening, I have just come back, and she is strung up, she has got a rope around her neck." He summoned a neighbour, who was a nurse, for help. As the neighbour checked for a pulse, Longworth sat on the stairs, cradling his wife and stroking her hair.

Police arrived and found Tina on the floor of the hallway, a photo of her children on either side of her body. Longworth, who worked as an ophthalmic technician at Specsavers laboratory in Southport, told police he had been out that evening celebrating his 37th birthday at the Southport Sailing Club, where he was top man, the commodore.

The next day's *Liverpool Echo* ran the headline: "Mum in tragedy". The story said a Merseyside mother had been found hanging while her children slept. "Police have this afternoon ruled out foul play," it stated. It quoted Detective Chief Inspector Neil McAteer: "Following the post-mortem this morning, we are happy that there are no suspicious circumstances. We will, however, continue our investigations."

Paul Longworth said the marriage was fine. His wife did not appear to be suicidal, he said, but added that she suffered from depression and had a morbid fear of cancer. The next morning he would sit their two children down and tell them, "Mummy got bad in the night. The doctor couldn't help. Mummy's gone to heaven."

Southport is a large seaside town on the Irish Sea, around 17 miles north of Liverpool. It is famous for its expansive beach, pier and Victorian architecture. Famed as a resort in the 19th century and retaining a genteel image, like many coastal locations in recent decades its past glories have faded, though the local newspapers frequently carry stories about plans to invest in and rejuvenate the town. Today, Southport has pockets of poverty, and once-bustling Lord Street with its glass canopies over the shopfronts has lost its bustle. However, the area around Southport includes England's golf coast – including the Royal Birkdale Golf Club – and is home to multi-millionaire footballers from Merseyside's Premier League clubs, Liverpool and Everton.

When news of the tragedy on Peel Street hit the headlines, it stunned Southport's Blowick neighbourhood, where people either knew or had at least seen the family with such nice children. It was hard to fathom how such misfortune could befall them. The Longworths looked so settled and normal. There was Paul with his good job and leading position in the sailing club, often the life and soul of the clubhouse. Tina was clearly a loving and devoted mother.

They had married seven years previously. People found Paul charming, and when Tina's family first met him they could see she thought he was lovely. She kept the household in an immaculate condition, in addition to doing three part-time jobs.

Police initially went along with Longworth's account of what had happened to Tina. When her body was later examined, however, 36 marks were found on it. The other curious factor was that she had not left a suicide note. The police decided to call in Home Office pathologist Dr Edmund Tapp to examine Tina, rather than the local pathologist.

HOME OFFICE
PATHOLOGIST
DR EDMUND TAPP

"The body had been taken to the hospital," Dr Tapp said. "I was at home and the police rang me and said that although it appeared to be a hanging, they were just a bit concerned. They'd like me to go and have a look at it and do the post-mortem. So I went to Southport and the puzzling thing about it, when I saw the body, was the fact that there wasn't just a hanging mark on the neck, there was a horizontal mark as well. And this made me begin to become suspicious as to whether it was indeed a straightforward hanging.

"The most prominent feature, in addition to the marks on the neck, were the large number of pinpoint haemorrhages on the face and the congestion of the face, which goes along with someone who's had compression on the neck. The other feature was bleeding in the eyes, which again is a feature of strangulation."

The face of a strangulation victim can appear congested, or bloated, and will have petechial haemorrhages, or pinpoint lesions. Petechial rashes around the eyes and mouth are more common[5] in strangulation than hanging.

"The point that I found interesting and made me wonder as to whether it was a strangulation was the fact that in addition to the pinpoint haemorrhages on the face, there were pinpoint haemorrhages on the neck in between the strangulation mark and the hanging mark. If this had just been a hanging, we would have only found the pinpoint haemorrhages above the hanging mark and not between the two."

Dr Tapp suspected that Tina may have been strangled and then hanged. He also noted that on Tina's neck there were scratch marks and bruises above the ligature mark. This suggested that in a struggle, if she was being strangled, Tina may have inflicted the marks on herself as she fought to relieve the pressure on her neck.

"In addition, there were a number of bruises on her arms," Dr Tapp said, "more than you would normally find. It suggested that she might well have been held. And finally, there were bruises on her legs. The fact that there were these other injuries on the neck and on the arms and legs suggested to me that this wasn't a straightforward suicide. There might well have been a struggle."

Detectives were present at the post-mortem. "Usually, the detective in charge of the case is present at the post-mortem examination," Dr Tapp said. "He or one of his officers takes notes for me, and then I use those as a basis for my report. And there's a continuous conversation between the pathologist and the senior investigating officer [SIO]. He will pass information to the pathologist; the pathologist will feed the SIO with his feelings as he goes along with the post-mortem." Dr Tapp indicated the marks on the body to the detectives and suggested these needed further investigation. His conclusion was that there were a number of suspicious circumstances in Tina's death that needed to be followed up. The police suggested he go to the Longworth home with them to inspect the scene of death. Paul Longworth was at the house when the police and pathologist arrived.

"He seemed quite calm and normal," Dr Tapp said. "You know, there was nothing remarkable about him." When Longworth asked if he should stay while Dr Tapp inspected the scene, the police told him to wait in the sitting room.

On looking over the hallway, Dr Tapp was puzzled by the lack of a mark on the banister spindle, suggesting there had not been a lot of movement or prolonged hanging. Now that the pathologist had outlined his doubts about this being a hanging, the police investigation entered a new phase.

There was another discrepancy. Two photos of the children had been found next to Tina's body, suggesting that in a state of distress that she had perhaps done away with herself but still wanted to keep her children close. But how had they come to rest beside her if she had hanged herself from the spindle, supposedly holding the photographs? The final arrangement of body and photos appeared to have been staged.

When it was also discovered that Tina had taken a contraceptive pill hours before her death, suspicions mounted further. Why would she do that if she was contemplating suicide?

Something else struck detectives in the aftermath of Tina's death. When interviewed by them, Paul Longworth seemed anything but distressed. "Fire away," he said.

TINA LONGWORTH WITH
HER GRANDFATHER
ON HER WEDDING DAY

Inquiries were made into the state of the Longworths' marriage. Paul Longworth's suggestion that the marriage was happy was soon shown to be untrue. In fact, the relationship had soured badly.

Longworth may have appeared charming and accomplished, but those who knew him revealed another side of his personality. A member of the sailing club,

Jane Johnson, said, "When you first met Paul you thought, 'What a charming bloke.' But later he made your skin crawl." Another said, "He loved being in a boat. Seeing him tack into the wind and zip across the water was special. But on dry land he was a rat."

He had joined the club in 1990 and was a keen weekend sailor. He was elected commodore in 1996. Before that, in the early 1990s, he and Tina would often sail together on Southport's Marine Lake, before they had their two children. Thereafter, Tina would often spend Sundays at the club, watching her husband on the water or playing with her children at the clubhouse.

Despite Tina's devotion to the children and the household, Longworth, who was a divorcé, had got bored with the relationship. He was overheard saying she was "an embarrassment".

On one occasion at a sailing event, Tina's boat capsized and she fell into the water. Longworth, who was watching from the club bar, said, "The only trouble is she's coming up."

A woman said, "Do you mean that?"

"I do," he replied.

Police suspected he had affairs, and he had a reputation as a lecher among sailing club members. At the club he followed one of Tina's friends into the toilet, kissed her and put his hand up her skirt. His disregard for Tina was glaring even after her death. Clinical forensic psychologist Professor Mike Berry said, "He was very insensitive to her and her memory. And there was a reported suggestion that he made sexual advances to some of her friends quite soon after her death.

So we had a situation where the man wasn't behaving the way you would anticipate with somebody who had been bereaved by the tragic death of his young wife."

Longworth was also violent. Two months before her death, Tina told best friend Sandra Ashcroft, "He's beaten me." Tina had also revealed that Longworth had forced her to have sex with him. Sandra told her that was rape. He had also once threatened to "break every bone in her body".

Emotional letters that Tina wrote in 1990, a year into the marriage, and left sealed and hidden in her jewellery box, may offer an insight into how desperate she was feeling early in the relationship. The letters, one to her husband and the other to four-month-old daughter Abby, were marked "Only to be opened in the event of my death". To Abby she wrote, "As I sit here writing this, you are sitting next to me in your bouncy chair chatting away to me. You will only be reading this if I have died.

"I just want you to know I love you and your daddy very much and I want you to look after him and make sure you welcome anybody that your daddy loves into your home. I know it will be hard to love a new mummy, but I am sure you will learn to love her and I will not think you are being disrespectful to me."

The letter to her husband read, "I just wanted you to know that I love you very much and Abby equally as much. Please take good care of her...

"Send all my clothes to Oxfam. Please keep all my jewellery and give it to our daughter on her 18th birthday.

"All I have left to say is goodbye. And I hope when you find someone new, she will not be as difficult as I was."

Miserable in a loveless marriage, Tina became friendly with the sailing club's rear commodore, fireman Gary Silcock, who was in his early forties. Silcock would say later that he fell for Tina because he felt sorry for her. "It was probably the wrong way to start a relationship," he said, but at first they just shared their problems. "We were two people who didn't really know what was happening to our lives. Tina and I seemed to give each other comfort."

The closeness between the pair was noticed at the sailing club and rumours started. The relationship became physical when Tina said to Gary, "Wouldn't it be nice if the rumours were true?"

Both Gary and Tina's marriages were in trouble. Gary's wife had told him the relationship was over. He and Tina started meeting several times a week for liaisons in his car at secluded beauty spots. Gary recalled, "I knew it was wrong, but when we met it was like another world. We would talk, laugh, go for picnics.

"Tina never made any demands on me. Although she didn't love Paul, she didn't want to hurt him." Silcock would later say in court, "She didn't want to leave Paul. She didn't want to hurt him, and she couldn't leave her children."

Longworth was spying on Tina. He checked the mileage when she used their car, and when he discovered unexplained miles clocked (from her meetings with Gary Silcock), he took away the car keys. She then faced a mile-long walk to playgroup with the children. He also fitted a phone-monitoring machine at home so he could check incoming and outgoing calls.

Striving to be as hurtful as possible, Longworth had not bought his wife any presents for her last Christmas a couple of weeks before her death. Tina was torn between struggling on in her marriage, perhaps for the sake of her children, and making a life for herself and the children with someone else.

She met Gary the day before she was murdered. "She was crying because Paul had called her a worthless piece of shit. I got annoyed and said, 'Tina, you cannot carry on like this. You have to leave him and go to your mum's or get a flat.' Tina just dismissed it."

After their last meeting, he said, "She never once spoke of killing herself."

Eventually, police pieced together what had happened in the Longworth home on Tina's last day alive. It was her husband's 37th birthday, but they had rowed in bed that morning. He would later admit that he ripped up her birthday card to him in front of her. He went to work, but on his return the argument continued.

Paul Longworth then went to a birthday celebration on his own at Southport Sailing Club. However, at some point, he snuck out, returned home and strangled Tina, before attempting to make it appear that she had hanged herself.

Semen stains were found on her nightie and it was suspected that he may have sexually assaulted Tina that evening, which could explain some of the marks on her body.

After looking at the case, Prof Mike Berry was struck by Longworth's arrogance: "He thought he was cleverer than the police. He thought that he was going to get away with it. And he convinced Tina's family that he was innocent and that it [the murder charge] was a tragic mistake. He kept that up for a very long time."

Having staged the "suicide", Longworth then went back to his birthday party at the club, hoping to use it as an alibi for his brutal attack on his wife. He bought drinks and put on a front as the birthday boy, centre of attention that evening.

Meanwhile, and in a further statement of his monstrous disregard not just for Tina but their children too, he left Abby and Matthew sleeping in a bedroom overlooking where their mother was dangling from the banister spindle.

Jackie Malton, former senior Metropolitan Police detective (and role model for DCI Jane Tennison in television's *Prime Suspect*), said, "What makes this crime particularly unpleasant and horrific is that in creating an alibi, he, in his selfishness, risked his very young children getting out of their bed and seeing their mother dead, hanging from the spindle, which would have traumatised them for life. Fortunately, they slept through it."

Criminal psychologist Dr Donna Youngs adds, "A key illustration of the way Paul Longworth's ego has gone out of control is that he is oblivious to the possibility that his little children

DR DONNA YOUNGS,
INVESTIGATIVE
PSYCHOLOGIST

may discover the body of their mother. This shows me that other people, even his own children, have ceased to register for Paul Longworth if his ego is damaged."

Dr Youngs has researched how offenders see themselves, pinpointing four narrative themes that help to drive criminal action – one of which is a "hero narrative" (the other narratives being professional, victim and revenger). This is the narrative she sees as being most useful in defining Longworth. "Paul Longworth is an unusual criminal. He was an eminently respectable, well socially integrated individual, which I think is why this case is so hard to process.

"But he is a classic example of how the hero narrative can go wrong and lead to violent criminality. Classic hero narrative sometimes go wrong when the ego grows out of control. Then nothing else matters but protecting that ego. The significance of the individual, their role and importance, and above all their pride, is paramount. It's not just that they don't care about other people, it's that other people just don't register as significant in their world. That's how Paul Longworth could do this to his wife, that's how he could leave the body where his little children could have potentially come across it."

Prof Mike Berry picks up on the theme of Longworth's self-interest and arrogance when faced with the possibility that Tina could leave him. "Paul Longworth was very much into image management. He wanted to create the image of being the commodore of the local sailing club, a man of some means and status. Having his wife run off with the fireman would have absolutely shattered that image. Had he been successful, he could then have had even more sympathy: *Poor man, his wife committed suicide.*"

Anger and possessiveness were driving him. "This wasn't an act of passion," Prof Berry said. "It was more an act of terror and punishment. And quite clearly, the way he put the rope around her neck and tied it and forced her down the stairs indicated a man who was very angry that she was considering leaving him."

Despite his apparent belief that he was too smart to be caught, Longworth made many mistakes in pretending that Tina had killed herself. In addition to the pathologist's doubts and his own unconvincing demeanour as a grieving husband, he made other blunders.

As Prof Berry pointed out, staging a murder to look like a suicide is difficult to achieve. "Often we take tablets or do something else," he said. "Hanging yourself from the stairs is difficult, to hang yourself from halfway down the stairs is near impossible. You don't have enough height to get the full effect of breaking your neck."

Longworth had an injury on his hands, which was clearly rope burns. He had a flimsy explanation for these.

"He tried to persuade the police that the injury was caused when he lifted her up after he found her," Prof Berry said. "He lifted up her body and he burned his hands on the rope. This is highly unlikely. The injuries were such that his hand would have been in contact with the rope for a much longer period of time than just lifting up her body.

"The whole process was badly managed by him. He was trying to be clever by saying he wasn't there, with an alibi of having drinks in the clubhouse. But clearly there was evidence to show that she had been dead for some considerable time before he phoned the ambulance."

* * *

Paul Longworth went on trial at Liverpool Crown Court. He pleaded not guilty.

The prosecution case, led by Henry Globe QC, was that Paul Longworth had sexually assaulted Tina before strangling her from behind with a knotted length of sailing rope. He then attempted to make it look like she had hanged herself. Police believe he may have given the children a strong cough mixture at bedtime to help ensure they did not wake while he hanged his wife or during the time he was out. They slept throughout the upheaval as ambulance crew and police arrived.

Among the witnesses called was consultant clinical psychologist Dr Mary Jackson, who treated Tina for her cancer phobia. She said Tina was not suicidal. She was devoted to her children and her phobia was actually about wanting to live.

The prosecution argued that if Tina had been contemplating suicide, she would have confided this in her detailed and personal diaries, which she kept hidden from her husband. However, she made no reference to killing herself in them.

A work colleague and friend of Tina's, Tammy Rigby, testified that she met Paul Longworth at the sailing club, and he had tried to start an affair with her several times.

It also emerged that Longworth suspected Tina was having an affair with Gary Silcock and was planning to leave him. David Smith, Longworth's workmate at Specsavers, told the court that the accused had admitted that he hit his wife and that Tina accused him of raping her. He also said Longworth had joked that he could kill his wife by putting a pillow over her face when she had an asthma attack. Silcock testified about his affair with Tina.

After pathologist Dr Edmund Tapp had originally raised doubts that Tina committed suicide, a dispute between pathologists arose, which may have given Longworth some hope of casting doubt on his guilt. Dr Tapp recalled, "My findings were a description of the injuries that she sustained and the fact that they were more consistent with being due to strangulation, followed by hanging, rather than due to hanging. And, of course, in cases like this, other pathologists become involved because I was somewhat doubtful as to whether it was a suicide or a strangulation. They asked Dr [James] Burns, the pathologist for Merseyside at that time, to come and examine the body with me. And he, in fact, didn't agree with me. He felt that it was more likely to be just a hanging, and he gave evidence for the defence in the trial."

However, Dr Iain West, who was the director of forensic medicine at Guy's Hospital in London and an internationally recognised expert on hanging, concurred with Dr Tapp. His opinion was more forthright than Dr Tapp's. He testified that the horizontal mark that Dr Tapp had recorded at the original post-mortem was caused by someone strangling Tina with a ligature, before suspending her from the banister spindle.

"I think that Dr West's evidence certainly played an important part in him [Longworth] being found guilty," said Dr Tapp.

Longworth admitted when he testified that he tied the knot in the sailing rope that killed his wife, but added there were many such ropes in their house and they were used for several reasons.

Dressed in a blue suit and tie, he told the jury all was normal at home on the morning his wife died, though he would admit under questioning that he had ripped up his wife's card to him. Their seven-year-old daughter, Abby, had even got involved, shouting at her father, "You've ruined the day – you always do."

This had been his second marriage, Longworth told the court, his first having ended when he began an affair with Tina. He even became tearful when describing how he broke the news of Tina's death to the children. The prosecution, however, demanded to know why Tina had taken her contraceptive pill before she died.

"She took that pill because it was a normal night and she was going to bed," said the barrister Henry Globe. "You strangled her, didn't you?"

Longworth denied it.

The three-week trial reached a climax at the end of February 1998, when the jury of six women and four men, after four hours of deliberation, unanimously found Paul Longworth guilty of murdering Tina. Even now he stuck to his insistence of innocence – turning to the jury, according to a TV news reporter, and mouthing the words, *No, you're wrong.*

He received a life sentence. Mr Justice Hidden said, "You snuffed out the life of your wife for your own selfish reasons without any regard for your two children. You passed yourself off as a good father, but your taking away of their mother was a callous, violent act.

"The dreadful loss you have inflicted on your children will remain with them for the rest of their lives."

Another act of cruel duplicity Longworth had committed was to completely deceive some members of Tina's family into believing he was innocent. They sat in stunned silence as the guilty verdict was read out.

Afterwards, Tina's friend Sandra Ashcroft, who had lunched with her on the day of her murder, said, "If she had wanted to kill herself she would have done it away from her children – not just yards from where they were sleeping. She lived for her children, Abby and Matthew. Nothing would have made her hang herself outside their rooms."

She described Tina as shy, but caring and intelligent. Sandra also offered a telling insight into the nightmare of her relationship with Paul Longworth. "Paul saw Tina as his possession. He was always telling people that he didn't want her, but the thought of someone else having her drove him mad."

Detective Inspector Bob Morrison said after the verdict, "Paul Longworth has been described as a ruthless and callous individual. The murder he committed and his actions since have proved that description to be true. Although I am obviously pleased with the result, the reality of today is that two young children have, in effect, lost their father as well as their mother."

He added that he had been surprised members of the dead woman's family had supported Longworth throughout the trial, but concluded that was testament to how plausible the killer's lies had been.

Tina's grandmother, Phyllis Brannan, 73, said: "At first Paul was nice to Tina, but he turned and showed his true colours.

"He has destroyed a beautiful person and deprived two innocent children of a wonderful mother. If there was hanging, I would pull the trapdoor myself."

Little Matthew would tell the boys and girls at his nursery, Scarecrows, that his mother had become a star in the night sky. In memory of Tina they sang *Twinkle, Twinkle, Little Star* and the staff would have to bite their lips. Alison Cotterall, who founded the nursery, knew Tina and Paul. After the trial she was also insistent that the young mother would never have taken her own life: "We all knew what a doting mum Tina was and knew she would not kill herself." When the news broke of her death on the radio, Alison said, "We all looked at each other and said, 'He's killed her.'"

In 1999 the three detectives who had built the case against Longworth won commendations. It turned out that Det Insp Morrison and his colleagues Detective Sergeant John Belger and Detective Constable Richard Forshaw had pursued the case despite the misgivings of their superior officer. Belger said they had had doubts about Longworth's account from day one, but overcoming opposition from above had not been easy. Despite the obstacles, they had painstakingly amassed the evidence to convict him.

The fallout of Longworth's appalling crime would continue for the children. Some 10 years after the trial, Abby, who was aged 16 at the time, made a shocking discovery. She had Googled her name one day, expecting to discover fun pictures of herself out with friends. What she found instead were news stories revealing that her father had murdered her mother. As she told the *Daily Mirror* in 2011 when she was 21, she had never been told what had happened. "It was horrifying," Abby told the paper. "I couldn't tear my eyes away from the newspaper reports. It was as though I was reading about someone else's life and not mine." She was taken aback and could not tell anyone what she had learned. Her memories of Tina were fleeting, but she retained a clear feeling that she and her brother, who was 19 at this time, had been cherished and loved by their mother.

"Mum worked at a school nursery and if I was sick she took me to work with her, tucked me into one of the sick beds and gave me lots of kisses and cuddles," she remembered.

She believed she had a recollection of her parents arguing on the night her mother was murdered. She had crept on to the landing, but her father ordered her back to bed. In the morning, Abby woke to find her mother's half-sister, Sarah, sitting on the bed edge. She had been sobbing. She told the children her mother was gone and they would be living with her for a while. Abby thought that somehow there had been a mistake and that her mother would eventually reappear. "It never occurred to me she was dead," she said.

Instead, later that year, Sarah told Abby her father was in jail (he was awaiting trial). Confused, she felt she could not ask questions, that there was some cloak of secrecy that the adults would not breach. Her grandmother took her to the prison to see her father, but she found this unpleasant and frightening. She and her brother had no idea why he was there. Sarah and the family moved to an area of Manchester to escape events in Southport.

When Abby was 14, social workers told her and her brother that their father had killed Tina. Because she always assumed her parents had been happy together, Abby now felt her mum must have been the victim of a fatal accident. She tried to shut out the constant questions about the past and stopped visiting her father.

However, after the shock of the Google search, Abby was determined to finally learn what had happened to her mother. In October 2009 she visited her father again in Stafford Prison. "Dad seemed so haggard," she recalled. "But I didn't let that put me off and as soon as I sat down – I demanded to know why he'd killed Mum." She was dismayed when her father denied killing her mother. She said, "There was no remorse or sorrow, just more lies and betrayal. I was sick of it and stormed out of the prison."

She wrote to the parole board and said that despite the judge recommending that Longworth should spend at least 14 years in jail, her father had expressed no remorse to her and should serve a full life sentence.

Despite the pain of learning what had happened to her mother, at least the children could face the future without nagging questions and uncertainty. Abby resolved to embrace her future for the sake of Tina. She and Matthew remained close.

JOHN COOPER

Pembrokeshire Coastline

3

"It was important the jury understood they were dealing with a cold executioner"

Pembrokeshire coast, 1985–2009
Victims: Helen and Richard Thomas, Peter and Gwenda Dixon, and many more
Murderer: John Cooper

Bullseye was a mainstay of ITV's Sunday afternoon schedules during the 1980s and 90s. The darts-themed gameshow with a quiz element featured three pairs of contestants competing for cash and prizes, from cars and speedboats to consolation goodies – a tankard, a goblet, or perhaps a Bendy Bully toy replica of the show's mascot. At the highpoint of its success, the show was watched by 20 million viewers.

In an episode recorded on 28 May 1989, a Welshman called John Cooper appeared on it. With a mullet hairstyle and moustache of the kind popular with footballers at the time, Cooper spoke quietly to the host, comedian Jim Bowen. Cooper was right at home with the pub culture celebrated by the show. He was well known in his local, liked darts and had signed up for the show with another member of the pub's darts team.

When introducing the contestants, Bowen (catchphrase: "You can't beat a bit of Bully") asked Cooper about his "unusual hobby".

"Oh yes, the scuba diving," Cooper replied.

"Scuba diving, and apparently it's the place to do it?" Bowen was referring to the Pembrokeshire coast, where Cooper was born and still lived.

"Oh, we've got the coastline."

"Yes, because the mountains are sort of inverted and you've got all these…"

"We've got deep water where you swim over mountains and all sorts of things," Cooper says, appearing rather diffident.

This appearance on primetime television, before millions of viewers, would later astonish detectives of the Dyfed-Powys force. *Bullseye*, with its jaunty theme tune and light-hearted gags, was an incongruous setting in which to find Cooper. He was not a jaunty, light-hearted kind of guy. He was a sadist, violent robber and murderer of a defenceless brother and sister who lived locally to him.

"You would have thought he would want to keep a low profile," said clinical forensic psychologist Professor Mike Berry. "You go on television, if you become famous even for 15 minutes, then the media will take some interest in what you're doing. And I would have thought that would give him the attention that he didn't want. But it also shows how calm he was. That he could actually go on the programme having already committed murders and not bat an eyelid. Clearly, he has all the characteristics of a psychopath."

Within weeks of recording *Bullseye*, Cooper would commit another horrendous double murder, and later traumatise a group of teenagers, raping one young woman and assaulting another. Jim Bowen and ITV would have been aghast to know the truth about the man they were welcoming on to this family show.

Cooper was an arrogant risk-taker, a gambler, and clearly thought he was too smart to be caught by police. Perhaps that's why he paraded himself on national television despite being wanted for a catalogue of violent burglaries and murders. However, if he was expecting to be a big success on *Bullseye* with plenty to crow about down the pub later, he was to be disappointed. He was a flop in the quiz section of the game, shown up by a female contestant next to him who was faster on the buzzer and knew the correct answers. He cracked a smile, but inside he would have seethed at being beaten by a woman.

Then he had an opportunity to restore some pride in the face of humiliation. For *Bullseye's* finale, the winners got the chance to gamble prizes they had won so far against a hidden star prize. If the winners declined, the runners-up were given the chance to risk their prizes. This time the test was at the dartboard rather than answering quiz questions, and it was Cooper's turn to throw.

This was his zone, where his prowess would prevail. He strode to the oche, the drums rolled – and Cooper lost everything. Jim Bowen patted him on the arm, making a consoling joke, but Cooper was unlikely to have taken the loss with sporting good cheer.

John William Cooper was born in Milford Haven on 3 September 1944. He left school at the age of 15 and married his late wife, Patricia, in 1966, the couple having two children, a boy and a girl. He trained in upholstery and carpentry, worked as a farm labourer and in the building trade, with periods of unemployment in between.

It was in 1978 while working as a welder's mate on the Gulf Oil Refinery at Milford Haven that Cooper hit the jackpot. He won £90,000 (the approximate equivalent of £530,000 today) in a newspaper spot-the-ball competition, along with an Austin Princess car worth £4,000 (£23,000 today). He was suddenly rich, the win having changed his life.

Unfortunately for Cooper's family, he was too reckless to enjoy the benefits of this windfall for long. He lost money on a series of house moves and through gambling. Within a couple of years he had frittered his winnings away.

He also had a history of lawbreaking from an early age and was a violent man. Police think that by 1983 he had started burgling homes. He was a prodigious housebreaker and would eventually be convicted of 30 break-ins, but he was linked to many more. He fancied himself as an outdoorsman and something of a survivalist, watching survival programmes on TV and keeping a copy of the SAS handbook. As a keen fisherman and local of the area around Milford Haven, set in the beautiful Pembrokeshire coastal area, he had intimate knowledge of the pathways and fields nearby. He would roam the fields at night, watching houses, planning which to attack.

Cooper was not what might once have been called a cat burglar, slipping in and out of properties. He took a shotgun with him and was not put off by encountering the residents. In one incident, he threw a television at the head of a victim, kicked and tied up the homeowners, and kept returning to them to hit them with the butt of his gun.

Prof Mike Berry gives an insight into how Cooper stood out from most burglars. "Normally, burglars are very efficient when they're committing burglaries," he explained. "If we exclude the ones who get drunk in the pub and go afterwards to commit a burglary, a proper burglar will check the area where he's going to go in, knowing exactly what he wants. He will quickly find a point of exit and then go around the house, farmyard or building, get what he wants and out. Many, many burglars will be in and out in a few minutes. The other thing is, they're often very highly aroused about time because it is dangerous. It is a risk that they could get caught, especially as they often break into houses at night when people are actually sitting there watching television, and that's always a risk… but there's also the excitement, the buzz. It's easy to do. You go in, get what you want and out quickly.

"Lots of burglars will never get into violence, most will try to avoid it. But here we've got a man that's gone from burglary into robbery, and he's being violent to get hold of the goods he wants. We eventually get to a situation where he escalates it to actually robbing and killing."

Three days before Christmas in 1985, Cooper targeted a manor house three miles outside Milford Haven. Scoveston

Park was the Georgian home of wealthy siblings Richard and Helen Thomas. On this wet and windy night, at around 11pm, flames were seen coming from the direction of the house. By the time emergency crews got there it was obvious that if anyone was inside the building, they would not have survived the inferno. A strong smell of petrol was noticed by the firefighters. Just after midnight the body of Richard Thomas was recovered from the burnt-out property. A wound was evident on the right side of his abdomen. An x-ray showed that it contained lead shot. Scoveston Park was now a murder scene, and the priority became to find and preserve evidence.

The building's wooden floors had burned through and collapsed, but Helen Thomas's body was eventually found on the ground floor in a poor condition. X-rays revealed that she had also been shot, lead particles being found in what remained of the bottom of her skull.

The deaths were shocking because they were so out of character for this quiet area. Richard, aged 58, owned a lot of land and had followed his father into farming. Both he and his sister, who was 54, were rather reserved. Though they were wealthy, the idea that they had been targeted by a violent gang just seemed too alien in this part of the world. The possibility of a murder and suicide was considered. Had there been a rift between Helen and Richard?

The post-mortems shifted the theories away from murder-suicide. Helen's body was tied with black rope, and around her neck was a bloodstained shirt with sleeves knotted. It seemed to investigators that she had been bound and gagged or blindfolded. Now a burglary that got out of hand was considered. The property was thoroughly searched and no shotgun could be found, further ruling out any element of suicide. Detectives realised they had a brutal double murder on their hands. It was going to be a grim Christmas for officers drafted in to assist with the case. Normally Dyfed-Powys Police dealt with an average of two murders a year, and these were often of a domestic nature. Crime rates were low in North Pembrokeshire, an area of outstanding natural beauty that relied on tourism and farming for its income. The Scoveston Park murders had shattered the local sense of pastoral charm and safety.

An incident room was set up, and scene-of-crime officers and forensic experts sifted the debris. It soon became clear the killer had taken his shotgun and discharged cartridges away with him after setting fire to the house. Further searching advanced the detectives' understanding of what had occurred. On Boxing Day a pool of blood and lead pellets were found in an outbuilding behind the main house. It looked as though Richard had returned to the house, been confronted by the intruder, and had been shot. His body was then moved to the house. When the bodies were re-examined it was found that Richard had, in addition to the abdominal gun wound, also suffered a glancing shotgun blast to the side of his head.

Because the level of violence was senseless and out of proportion to the normal pattern of a burglary, it confounded the police. It was a challenge to work out what, if anything, might have been stolen from the property. However, the value of any stolen belongings was impossible to reconcile with the appalling level of brutality and carnage inflicted here. Richard was even found to have £75 in his pocket. Had the Thomases recognised the intruder, who then felt they must be silenced with a shotgun blast? Would someone local commit such savage murders? Was this the work of a band of travelling, ruthless criminals?

The local police faced the biggest investigation in the force's history. Houses and farms in the locality were visited and residents' movements recorded, road checks were used to question motorists, and a £25,000 reward was offered for information on the killings. Some 70,000 statements were taken, more than 100 people questioned, but all detectives were left with was a theory: this was a robbery of a woman at home alone that went wrong when Richard Thomas returned home unexpectedly. Helen witnessed all this, and the intruder lost control of the situation and killed them both.

John Cooper got away with this brutal double murder – for several years, at least.

Prof Berry emphasised that Cooper's homicidal violence in response to this situation was extremely rare. "Most people who commit robberies will not escalate into murder," he said. "We don't know why Cooper escalated. He may not even know, but we know that he was used to carrying guns." Burning down the house may have been punitive, his backlash to having been thwarted during the robbery by Richard Thomas, or simply his determination to destroy evidence and avoid capture. "And it obviously worked," said

Prof Berry. "He wasn't actually convicted for many, many years for this offence. He then went on robbing."

It is worth looking more closely at the kind of man Cooper was. Steve Wilkins, the detective superintendent who ended up heading the team that would eventually snare Cooper, built up detailed knowledge of his criminal activities. He said the sadistic killer started out as a peeping tom who moved on to burglary, robbery and finally murder. Cooper used his intimate knowledge of the fields and paths around Haverfordwest to plan his break-ins carefully. His preparations included cutting holes in fences for his escape. He would attack women who lived in houses that backed on to fields. Once he was confronted by homeowners, he turned violent. Wilkins believes the control he gained over victims and the disproportionate violence he used aroused him sexually. Valuables that he took would pay for his gambling habit. Much of what he took, however, was worthless, being what criminologists call "trophies", kept and used by serial offenders to relive the thrill of their crimes. For example, police would later find 500 sets of keys hidden in a cesspit on Cooper's land, some of which would be matched to keys stolen during his burglaries.

The former detective also described Cooper as having a very inflated opinion of himself and his abilities. On winning the £98,000, he decided to become a turkey farmer. The venture was an immediate failure. He bought a £2,000 racehorse, which he transported on the motorway in a cheap horse box with a rotten floor. The horse fell through and shattered its legs. Such debacles were always blamed on someone else.

Gareth Rees, a detective sergeant who was on the case, said, "He was a nasty individual even in the family environment. He lived on a farm and he killed a pig... with a hammer. And when his children were small, they reared some chicks and he shot them with a shotgun in front of them."

Cooper was violent towards his son, Adrian – who changed his name to Andrew. The boy grew up petrified of his father. He left the family home at the age of 16 and had little contact with his family for five years. He would also later testify in court that his father often went for long evening walks with a shotgun under his coat. He said John Cooper kept photographs, trinkets and jewellery in a metal cupboard, all apparently the belongings of other people. Cooper was described by Andrew as very strong, very fit and a "loud, aggressive man". Quite a difference from the modest front Cooper presented on *Bullseye*.

It was four years after he murdered the Thomases – and just four weeks since his *Bullseye* appearance – that Cooper's vicious rage erupted into homicide again. The crime was discovered after Tim Dixon and his sister, Julie, visited their parents' home in Oxfordshire on 3 July 1989 and found they had not returned from holiday. Peter and Gwenda Dixon had been on their annual summer trip to Little Haven village on the coast in North Pembrokeshire. This was a place the elder Dixons were devoted to and had visited for 15 years. Tim and Julie were surprised their parents had not yet returned.

Surprise turned to worry when it was learned that Peter was also absent from work. Tim called the owner of Howelston Farm Caravan Park, where the couple were staying, to ask about them. The Dixons were known by many local residents, having often walked and explored the clifftops and coves along the coast. The Dixons' Ford Sierra and their tent were still in the caravan park. It was learned that they had last been seen several days before, on 29 June, their last day booked at the site. Police were alerted. Search teams, dog handlers and a helicopter scoured the coast and area around the caravan park.

Finally, on 5 July, a police dog handler saw swarms of flies and a strong smell coming from near the cliff edge, below the path between Little Haven and Borough Head. The decomposing bodies of Peter, aged 51, and Gwenda, 52, were found in undergrowth. Broken branches had been used to cover them. Anyone walking along the coastal path would not have seen them. Detective Chief Superintendent Don Evans, who had also worked on the Scoveston Park investigation, recalled the moment the Dixons were found: "I heard, 'Boss, boss, come quickly.' My heart jumped and I ran along the coastal path to the dog handlers. There I saw this horrible scene. Peter and Gwenda Dixon – Peter shot, tied, and his dear lady, partly unclothed. Shot. The most horrific sight you've ever seen. It was an assassination. Here we had another double murder in Pembrokeshire. Horrific."

Professor Bernard Knight, Home Office pathologist, was summoned. "I remember staggering along the cliff path towards this spot, out in the wilds, really, above Little

PROFESSOR BERNARD
KNIGHT, HOME OFFICE
PATHOLOGIST

Haven. The path went along the top of this cliff, above what you might call the plateau, which is the top of the cliffs, but very heavily overgrown. I remember clambering down to this rather small area of grass between the bushes. By then, the people had been there trying to recover bodies with ropes and the usual paraphernalia of a crime scene.

"I was asked to look at these two bodies and I said no way. Because it was right on the edge of the cliff and one body was over the cliff edge. It was roped up so it couldn't fall any further. I couldn't actually see the body at first, but they dragged it up a bit further. I think the one that was furthest down was Gwenda Dixon. And the bodies – this was right in the middle of summer – were going off a bit, to say the least. Mr Dixon was higher up. But they were on a very dangerous place – it was 200 feet further down to the rocks and sea. One of the shakiest crime scenes I've been to, really."

It would become clear that both Peter and Gwenda had each been shot with a double-barrelled sawn-off shotgun, suffering multiple and very destructive pellet wounds. Peter had three gunshot wounds, including one to the head, and Gwenda two. Cooper would have reloaded the weapon twice during this cold-blooded annihilation. He had, once again, been careful to collect all the spent cartridges. Gwenda had also been sexually assaulted. The couple's belongings and the contents of their rucksack had been thrown around the scene. Peter's wallet was missing, as was his gold wedding ring.

As anyone who watches TV crime dramas will know, the first question detectives will ask a pathologist is about the time of death. Both bodies were infested with maggots, so entomologist Dr Zakaria Erzinclioglu of Cambridge University's Zoology Department was asked to examine the insects. "He was known as Uncle Zack," Prof Knight said, "and he was pretty hot at taking the life history of these various flies and bluebottles and whatever, and calculating from that how long they [the victim] were likely to have been dead." His calculation, along with the account of a witness who had heard five shots fired while walking on the beach below, indicated that the Dixons had been killed on the morning of 29 June.

Various theories were floated as to who could be behind such a grotesque double killing. While a major incident room was set up and Dyfed-Powys Police got to grips with a new Home Office Large Major Enquiry System computer (HOLMES), there were rumours that the IRA or drug runners may have crossed paths with the Dixons. Prof Knight said, "It was well known that there were landings of arms on the Pembrokeshire coast and certainly lots of landings of drugs. I had a cottage there for many years, a bit further up the coast, and that's where they caught people who had made a bunker on the beach and stored all these drugs, which had been imported from North Africa, I think. So, that sort of thing was suggested for this one, that perhaps the Dixons had disturbed somebody up to no good. And it could either be drugs or possibly IRA. And, in fact, there turned out to be a cache of IRA weapons and explosives, but it was nothing to do with this case."

However, the investigation got a strong lead when Peter Dixon's stolen cash card was used on four occasions following the murders. In a series of cashpoint withdrawals in Pembroke, Carmarthen and Haverfordwest, a total of £310 was withdrawn. Either Cooper had found the PIN number on a piece of paper, or he had forced Peter Dixon to reveal it.

It is difficult not to feel appalled and dismayed that Cooper had inflicted unspeakable trauma and injuries on two unassuming holidaymakers for the sake of a sexual assault, a gold ring and £310. One of the victims had been forced to witness the murder of the other, knowing they would be next.

"Does he get more out of killing?" Prof Berry asked. "He didn't seem to be scared of it. He seems to be quite happy to use violence to get what he wants, which is classic psychopathic behaviour. He's goal-orientated for what he needs and doesn't care about the consequences or the implications of what he's doing."

Cooper's senseless brutality had subverted the peace and sense of security enjoyed by local residents and visitors to this idyllic stretch of coast. It was now a place of trepidation and fear, where people were wary of strangers and made sure to lock their doors.

He would not be arrested for the two double murders for another 20 years, but Cooper had already made mistakes that would help to incriminate him. For example, he had been spotted by a motorist as he used Peter Dixon's cash card in Haverfordwest. He was described as being five feet ten inches tall, late thirties to early forties, collar-length hair, unshaven with a moustache, wearing ankle boots and khaki-brown shorts. An artist's impression of the "wild man" was produced and shown on the BBC's *Crimewatch* programme, which later would help to incriminate Cooper.

For now, however, he evaded a massive police hunt – despite almost being implicated at one point. It was discovered that a gold ring had been sold at a jeweller's in Pembroke. If this had been Peter Dixon's ring, the person who sold it could obviously be the killer. Detectives checked with the jeweller and his records showed it had been sold by a "J Cooper". A detective constable spoke to Cooper. His story was that it was his own wedding ring that he had sold. Patricia, his wife, confirmed this. The detective did not feel Cooper resembled the artist's impression. Cooper had lied his way out of capture. The investigation went cold.

Unfortunately, Cooper was able to rampage and devastate the lives of more innocent victims. On 6 March 1996, five youngsters aged 14 to 16, were strolling through the fields near the Mount council estate on the edge of Milford Haven. The three girls and two boys were messing around by a tree with a rope swing in a wood. Later, with the light fading, they set off to return home on the estate. They were stopped by someone shining a bright light at them across a field. They thought it might be a friend. Then they realised the man closing in on them was wearing a balaclava and carrying a shotgun. He ordered them to lie on their stomachs. He raped a 16-year-old girl and assaulted a second girl, aged 15. The man demanded to know if they had any money. He told them not to reveal to anyone what he had done or he would kill them. As he walked away he fired the shotgun into the air. The youngsters hurried away and on reaching the home of one of the girls, they telephoned the police.

If a masked predator with a shotgun, intent on murder and sexual abuse, could roam the spaces around Milford Haven, no one was safe. This time Cooper had quelled a group of five youngsters to indulge his vicious need to exert control and traumatise others. Once again, a police incident room was set up in Haverfordwest. Police, well aware that the area was plagued by a wave of burglaries and robberies of lone women, in addition to the two unsolved double murders, interviewed suspects and checked leads, but again the investigation lost momentum. Scoveston Park and the coastal path murders remained painful, ongoing wounds for police and the community during these years.

Cooper, through ruthless deviousness and a little luck, had evaded detection despite multiple burglaries, robberies, murders and sexual attacks over more than a decade. However, his good fortune was about to run out – at least as far as his burglaries were concerned. A woman called Sheila Clarke was watching the telly in her bungalow in Sardis, near Milford Haven, on a winter night in 1996. This was a few months after the five youngsters had been ambushed by the man in a balaclava. Now, it was Sheila Clarke who was confronted by the balaclava man, brandishing a sawn-off shotgun.

"Money, I want money," he shouted.

He battered her with the gun's butt, hitting her head and body. He marched her to the bedroom and tied her up. He began searching for jewellery. Sheila was expecting her husband to return home soon. The terrifying possibility of another double murder was averted when Sheila managed to hit the panic button on her home burglar alarm system. The intruder fled. A neighbour tried to intervene, but the gunman threatened him and set off over the fields.

At this point, fortune was on the side of the police. In the hedgerows of surrounding fields they found items dumped by the retreating attacker. These included a rope, fleece, balaclava, gloves and a double-barrelled shotgun – a complete home-invader's attack kit.

Operation Huntsman was launched to investigate the series of burglaries, and it finally closed in on a suspect who would be found to have possessions stolen in a number of past home raids. The suspect was John Cooper. During house-to-house inquiries, he had been obstructive and refused to give a DNA sample. However, two years before, a police dog handler had traced a scent from a burglary at Castle Hill Crescent to a field opposite Cooper's home in the parish of Jordanston. The Huntsman team were suspicious of the aggressive Cooper and, after months of further investigation, he was arrested. As he was led in for trial, he shouted to journalists that he had been "fitted up". The jury did not fall for it, and he was finally given a 16-year sentence in 1998, after being found guilty of 30 burglaries and an armed robbery. At this point, in terms of evidence, Cooper still remained unconnected to the murders of the Thomases and Dixons, and the assault on the five youngsters. Though he had been questioned about the murders, he admitted nothing, and for now the police had no positive leads linking him to the killings.

In 2005 Detective Chief Superintendent Steve Wilkins recommended a forensic review of Pembrokeshire's unsolved historic cases of 1985 and 1989. Wilkins was born in Liverpool in 1959. The Cooper investigation would become the biggest case of his career. A major concern for him and his team at this time was that John Cooper could be released from prison in the near future. If he was the murderer they were seeking, as had been suspected, it was highly likely that he would kill again. Since Cooper had been in prison, the robberies in the vicinity had ceased. The two double murders had featured elements of Cooper's mode of offending: shotguns and robbery. Wilkins' trepidation as Cooper came up for parole was understandable. Operation Ottawa was launched in January 2006, initially to scrutinise the forensic evidence from the past offences. If a case against Cooper could be mounted, it would likely be based on forensics. What was thought likely to be a six-month operation ended up lasting six years.

The Ottawa team built a detailed picture of the series of burglaries that had hit the Milford Haven area over more than a decade. In excess of 60 burglaries had been committed with a similar *modus operandi*, or plan of action. This pattern suggested a single offender who kept to and refined his strategy. There were also four robberies, starting in 1985, the year of the attack on the Thomases at Scoveston Park, and culminating in the break-in at Sheila Clarke's bungalow in 1996. Scoveston Park was the first to involve a gun. The attacks were always on lone women in isolated properties. After Scoveston Park the attacker always used a shotgun.

It was the geography of the burglaries that had originally put Cooper in the frame as a suspect and ended in his imprisonment for them. Wire fences that had been cut, and the direction in which tracker dogs had followed the intruder's escape routes had revealed that Cooper lived at the epicentre of the crime wave in Jordanston. Officers from Operation Huntsman had arrested him and found 3,800 items of property and evidence in and outside Cooper's home, such as ropes, jewellery, 500 keys taken from properties, and ammunition. A sawn-off shotgun was among the items.

The evidence gathered from Huntsman now became the focus of Operation Ottawa. Wilkins pulled in the help of a private company, LGC Forensics, which had already done important work on major cases, such as the murder of Rachel Nickell on Wimbledon Common, London, in 1992. Professor Angela Gallop was its director of science and innovation. An author and forensic expert with an international reputation, she said, "We received a call at my laboratory from Steve Wilkins, the senior investigator, asking if we could help with this case. We'd been building up a reputation for being quite successful with cold cases, and he'd obviously heard about that.

"I remember hearing about the coastal path murders because they were so horrific. I didn't remember the Milford Haven sexual assaults or the Scoveston murders.

"The first thing that I would have done after getting the call from Steve Wilkins was to assemble the right team to do this case. Forensic scientists are different, like people in other professions, and it's really important to have the right mix of skills in any team that's going to undertake this sort of investigation. And then the second thing is to understand the crime scene, because it's from the crime scene that you get your forensic opportunities.

"We pored over the police photographs taken at the time, had briefings from the police, and we would have read reports and witness statements to get a good understanding of what had gone on."

The police originally wanted Gallop's team to restrict themselves to looking for DNA. A lot of time was therefore spent doing this, focusing, for example, on the rope used to tie Peter Dixon's hands and his clothing. While DNA traces were found, there was not enough to, as Prof Gallop put it, "get your teeth into".

Eventually, the detectives lost patience with her scientists. Prof Gallop recalled, "Steve gave me a call and said, 'Angela, you and your team have been working on this case for, I don't know, 18 months, and you found absolutely nothing. You're complete rubbish, and I'm going to take

PROFESSOR
ANGELA GALLOP

it from you and give it to another forensic provider.' You can't really be any more offensive than that to a forensic scientist. And I thought, hang on a minute, we've only been doing DNA and there are lots of other things we can do. I have learned over the years that it's sometimes really important to look for something else. Of course, DNA is very popular because of the large statistics that can be applied to it.

"So I said to Steve, I'm coming down to see you and we're going to talk about this – don't do anything now. And so I went down to Fishguard [where Operation Ottawa was based in an empty suite of rooms belonging to the Port Office]. I had probably the most difficult discussion I've ever had with a group of police officers in my whole career. They were incredibly hostile and deeply disappointed in us. And I think all I could say was, 'Well, you've put us in a straitjacket. Let us try to look for some other evidence, you know, give us our wings a bit and we'll see if we can find something.'

"And he rather reluctantly agreed, and he said, 'All right, you can look for textile fibres, whatever it is you want to look for.' And so I thanked him very much and we parted on, I have to say, much better terms."

This was what Wilkins would later call "a watershed moment".

The scientists started scrutinising some old gloves that Cooper had left in hedgerows near his home, probably because he didn't want to keep anything incriminating in his house. When people come into contact with each other, it is likely that clothing fibres will be exchanged. This was the kind of evidence Prof Gallop's team were looking for.

She said, "Almost immediately we started finding matching fibres, particularly with one marvellous tatty old glove, whose exhibit number was BB109. I think that's imprinted on our brains now. BB109 was something special, but we found fibres to link the Dixons with this glove that was found in the hedgerows.

"That started a whole series of fibre findings, which ended up with a myriad of fibres that connected the Dixons with the stuff in the hedgerow, and also provided connections with the sexual assaults at Milford Haven and even the body of Richard Thomas in Scoveston, which was extraordinary. In that case, the house had been set on fire after the murder, making it more difficult to find evidential traces. But even there, if you look really hard and you're really imaginative about things, if there's evidence to be found, you usually do find traces of it. And so we ended up with an enormous mass of these textile fibres."

Even though Cooper had been a suspect up to now, the Ottawa team had been careful to keep an open mind about him to ensure they did not, as frequently happened in failed investigations, become fixated on the wrong man. However, the fibre evidence was making him a much stronger candidate.

Then came a major breakthrough. The irony was that while examining fibres they found traces of blood, which meant potential DNA evidence that they had failed to find earlier.

Prof Gallop said, "We were interested in a pair of shorts that had been recovered from his [Cooper's] old house some years beforehand [during Operation Huntsman]. We didn't have an awful lot of clothing from him to look at. But this pair of shorts interested us, and we were looking for textile fibres on them, which we found. We were looking on this sticky tape strip, which is how we recover surface debris like textile fibres from things like clothing. And we saw a tiny flake or two of what looked like blood. We tested it – I mean, it's microscopic – and it did indeed appear to be blood. And we DNA-profiled that and that looked like it matched Peter Dixon.

"I remember ringing Steve Wilkins to give him the news because he'd been saying, 'All I want is a golden nugget, that's all I want.' And he'd obviously been very pleased by the fibres. But they couldn't be described as being a golden nugget. Anyway, I got him on the phone and he was driving, and I said to Steve, 'I think you'd better pull in, because I've got some news for you.' And he said, 'OK, right, right. I'll just pull in.'"

When she told him the news, Wilkins simply said, "Angela, I love you."

As Prof Gallop recalls, "I said, 'We found some DNA profiling matches on the shorts and it matches Peter Dixon.' That was what he would describe as a golden nugget.

"Then we went back to the shorts, because if we'd found some blood on the tape from the shorts, there should be some left on the shorts themselves. And we found a tiny amount on the back of one of the legs. We then profiled that, and that again absolutely gave us a full profile matching Peter Dixon. So that was the beginning of the DNA evidence."

After three years of meticulous hard work, here was a forensic hit. The scientists then moved on to the shotgun. Found near Cooper's home in a hedge, it was connected to him by a screw discovered in his house that fitted it. Prof

Gallop's team noticed that the barrel had been painted black and that the paint was flaking.

"We put a bit of this debris under the microscope just to check," she said, "We noticed that when it was well lit, as it is under a microscope, that it had a strange reddish cast to it. Of course, that always excites our interest. And it wasn't long before we discovered that that was because there was some blood under the surface of the paint flakes. We profiled that, and that looked like it matched Peter Dixon. And we then stripped some of the paint off the barrels and found more actually on the surface of the barrels themselves underneath the paint, implying obviously that the blood got on there before they had been painted black. And we profiled that, and that was a DNA match with Peter Dixon."

Under questioning, Cooper decided to imply his son might be the culprit. If the khaki shorts had incriminating DNA on them, it could be his son who had worn them, he suggested. It must take a particularly depraved and callous mentality to attempt to get the son you had been abusive and violent towards for years to pay for your own monstrous crimes.

The DNA findings presented a new challenge for the forensic experts. "So, then we were interested in seeing whether there were any other traces that could show that they had been worn by John Cooper in particular, or his son," said Prof Gallop. "We looked at some staining in the fly area of the shorts and found a mixture of John Cooper and his wife, Pat, there. We looked at a handkerchief found in the pocket and we found DNA that would come from John Cooper on that.

And I think we also got some of what we call wearer DNA – basically, it's material that's transferred from the body when an item of clothing is worn against it, skin flakes and that sort of thing. We found that that also contained John Cooper's DNA. So we had quite a lot to suggest that it was John Cooper who had been wearing the shorts. And if you compare the results that we got with the DNA profile of his son, then there was nothing to suggest that his son was an alternative wearer."

The gloves, the shotgun, even the shavings from Cooper's shed floor, were all providing traces linking him to the murders. But there were still further questions about the shorts. They looked shorter than those illustrated in the identikit picture of the man at the cashpoint in Haverfordwest using Peter Dixon's bank card. The laboratory team noticed that the hem of the shorts had been taken up and whoever stitched it had done a professional job. It was also known that Cooper's wife had worked as a seamstress. They unpicked the hem, and a small stain was found inside. The DNA of this sample was tested and it was found to belong to Julie, daughter of the Dixons. While this at first was thought to be unhelpful to the case against Cooper, it was then remembered that the contents of the Dixons' rucksack had been thrown around the crime scene near the coastal path. This suggested Cooper may have got blood on himself firing five times at the Dixons, and helped himself to a fresh pair of shorts, which had previously been in contact with Julie.

Prof Gallop said, "That, in the end, seemed to be the most likely explanation, so interpreted in the light of what the crime scene can tell you, it actually provided another rather interesting twist to the evidence. But with things like that, the science is not going to be wrong, it's just you've got to understand what it means. So sometimes you're going to be brought up short by something and you're going to have to think about it more deeply. Anyway, it was an interesting extra bit of evidence that we found."

After setbacks and doubts, Prof Gallop's team had become one of the first to successfully use DNA to unlock a cold case. It was certainly one of the most important of her career. "I suppose it is one of the landmark cases," she said.

It was the forensic work that really made the lawyers pay attention to the possibilities of getting a conviction. Gerard Elias QC was the barrister brought in to assess the evidence for the Crown Prosecution Service. He was a big man, quietly spoken but confident, distinguished-looking with a wealth of silver-grey hair. He found that what initially looked like a decent circumstantial case was transformed by the forensic work. In addition to the shorts and shotgun

forensic evidence, traces of foliage and fibres from Cooper's gloves further linked him to the murder of the Dixons as well as the Milford Haven attack on the teenagers. "The cold case detectives who investigated this over a period of years went to endless lengths and, in my view, did a remarkably excellent job in

GERARD ELIAS QC

pulling together all the strange strands of evidence," said the barrister.

The case against Cooper included his proximity to the crimes – his home was within an easy distance of Scoveston and the coastal walk. He was known to walk and cycle around the area, and he had been convicted for burgling properties throughout.

And there was a witness. This is where Cooper's hubris in appearing on *Bullseye* finally betrayed him. The police had the "wild man" identikit description given by the witness passing the Haverfordwest cashpoint. Ottawa's officers needed to confirm what Cooper looked like back in 1989 around the time of the coastal path murders. During their inquiries they had heard about his *Bullseye* appearance, which had been recorded a few weeks before the coastal path attack. After a lot of digging and some luck, ITV had located the recording

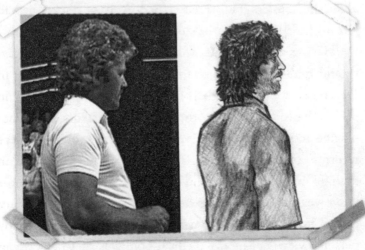

THE SIDE VIEW OF JOHN COOPER ON
BULLSEYE AND THE IDENTIKIT COMPARISON

from 20 years before. One still angle of Cooper on the show bore a striking similarity to the "wild man" with collar-length hair, moustache and shorts.

Elias, who showed the *Bullseye* footage of Cooper to the court during his trial, explained its significance: "Lo and behold, many years later, that description could be compared with a frame from the *Bullseye* programme on which Cooper himself had appeared. In similar profile, it showed what I'm sure the jury found ultimately to be compelling evidence that we were talking about the same man. So, here was another piece of the evidence – circumstantial, but an important piece of the evidence which tied Cooper to the murder."

Like the police, Elias was struck by Cooper's recklessness in appearing on television in front of millions of viewers. "An extraordinary performance, in my view, for a man who was at that stage committing the sort of crimes that he was, let alone the murders that were to come. And, of course, he had already killed the Thomases, unbeknownst then to anybody."

Having served 10 years of his 16-year sentence for burglary and robbery, Cooper was paroled and returned home in December 2008. As if the horror of this man's life had no end of harrowing twists, there then occurred yet another unexpected death. On the very first day of John Cooper's return to the family home, Pat Cooper, his wife, had had an evening meal with him, gone to bed and died. The post-mortem revealed she had three heart conditions that could have caused her death. As Det Ch Supt Wilkins said later, "My personal view, not in any medical books, is that Pat Cooper

gave up and could not face living with this man again."
She clearly dreaded the possibility of returning to the life
of physical and mental abuse she had suffered with Cooper
before he went to jail.

It was less than a month after the forensic breakthroughs
in April 2009 that Cooper was arrested for the two double
murders and assault on the five teenagers on 13 May. Gerard
Elias appeared for the prosecution in Cooper's trial, which
finally began at Swansea Crown Court on 21 March 2011.
Elias would later describe the accused's effect on the courtroom: "I think he came across as cold and calculating. He
was a man who from time to time would shout out to correct
a witness or to correct a proposition that maybe I was making
to the jury. He wanted to give the impression that it was all
rubbish and we shouldn't be listened to at all.

"Then he gave evidence himself. He sought to build up
a picture here that he was a family man living a normal life,
present at the wedding of his daughter, where he'd given her
away and so on." But later under cross-examination, Cooper
would be forced to admit several times that he was a liar.

"The stares that he would give," Elias continued, "the
stares he gave me when I was cross-examining him were there
for the jury to see. I don't think it did him any good. As he
would walk back and forth from the dock to the witness box
to give evidence, past the bench where I was sitting, he would
stare at me and I think the jury were aware of this. It was a
man who I think didn't believe that he could be stopped, that
he could be convicted – but ultimately, of course, he was."

Elias's priority in presenting the evidence against Cooper court was straightforward. "It was important the jury understood that they were dealing with a cold executioner," he said. "They were dealing with a man who would do anything to save his own skin. They were dealing with a man who took life for very, very little gain. I mean, the bank card in the Dixons case – he drew £50 two or three times from it. And a gold ring, which he sold for £25. He killed two people for that. It was never going to be more than a few hundred pounds. And it was important the jury understood they were dealing with a man for whom violence, for whom even killing, was just an occupational hazard."

The mountain of painstaking police and forensic work was distilled by the prosecution to demonstrate to the jury how Cooper carried out his crimes. Their case was that Cooper had gained access to Scoveston Park in the belief that Helen Thomas was alone. He tied her up and left her in an upstairs bedroom, when Richard Thomas returned home in his car. Richard was attacked and killed in an outbuilding and dragged into the main house. Cooper had done labouring work at Scoveston Park years before, so was almost certainly known to the Thomases. Helen may even have recognised his voice if he had been wearing a mask. Cooper had then used an accelerant, probably diesel, found on the property, to set ablaze the main building containing the bodies.

Regarding the Dixons, the prosecution said that Cooper, armed with a shotgun, had confronted the couple during their walk and forced them off the coastal path. He took them to a secluded spot around 15 yards from the path, where he forced Peter Dixon to give him his PIN number and sexually assaulted Gwenda. He killed the couple with multiple shotgun blasts and searched their belongings. He then covered the bodies with foliage and branches.

Investigators had also uncovered a fibre link between the rape and indecent assault during the Milford Haven attack and the gloves Cooper threw away fleeing from the Sardis burglary on Sheila Clarke's bungalow.

Within minutes of rising to cross-examine Cooper, Gerard Elias had dramatically got the accused to agree he had lied to the court during his previous trial for the burglaries. On that occasion he had denied that the balaclava abandoned after the raid on Sheila Clarke's home was his. Yet during this latest trial, and thanks to a hair found in the balaclava linking it to Cooper, he had had to acknowledge it actually was his. So, Elias asked, had he lied? Squirming, Cooper had to agree that he had. Elias went on to demonstrate that Cooper was a compulsive liar. It was really by then a question of what his explanations were as to the DNA. Here, despite defence attempts to suggest forensic evidence might have been contaminated, the police officers and forensic experts were robust in standing up for their painstaking work.

"I think the jury were out for a couple of days," said Elias. "Not surprising, given the amount of evidence they would have had to go through, and they came back and convicted Cooper of all counts: the murders as well as the robberies of the younger people and the rape of the 16-year-old.

"Cooper's reaction was – as it had been through the early part of the trial – to immediately start shouting that the jury had not been made party to some of the evidence in the case, that it was all a miscarriage of justice, and he wasn't there to listen to it anymore and so on. And indeed, he even tried to shout the judge down when the judge was passing sentence on him."

On 26 May, Cooper was sentenced to life imprisonment. He was 66 years old.

Elias's abiding memory of confronting Cooper in court was the psychopath's stare, which was saying in effect, *I can intimidate you too.* "The stare, the coldness," he said. "Here you are prosecuting me, but you'd better be careful."

Outside Swansea Crown Court, the victims' families paid tribute to their lost loved ones. Richard and Helen Thomas's family said they were devastated by the murders and had been plagued for years over why the Thomases had been attacked. The brother and sister had been much loved by their extended family, who had "missed out on their involvement and kindness".

Just before the trial, one of the young women terrorised by Cooper with her four friends died. She never saw him brought to justice.

Julie Ann Pratley, Gwenda and Peter Dixon's daughter, said her parents were irreplaceable and "had wisdom, humour and were compassionate".

Chief Superintendent Steve Wilkins said Cooper was a "very dangerous and evil man".

He stole to support his gambling addiction. He was also a psychopath, sadistic in his desire to control and terrorise those around him. As Prof Mike Berry said, Cooper was fixated on what he wanted. The pain and innocence of others did not stand in his way if wanted their belongings, a few hundred pounds off them, or to abuse them sexually.

Two chilling facts about Cooper remain. First, we may never know the full extent of his crimes.

Second, after his arrest in May 2009 for the double murders and the attack on the teenagers, police searched Cooper's car. In the boot they found rope and a pair of woollen gloves. Officers also discovered that he had ordered an Ordnance Survey Map of South Pembrokeshire. It would appear John Cooper had been planning a new wave of horror across the estuary.

ROBERT MOCHRIE

Barry

4

"Robert was the guy who wouldn't hurt a fly"

Barry, South Wales, 2000
Victims: Catherine Mochrie, James Mochrie,
Luke Mochrie, Sian Mochrie, Bethan Mochrie
Murderer: Robert Mochrie

The house at 43 Rutland Close was quieter than usual on the morning of Wednesday, 12 July 2000. Robert Mochrie was getting on with a few chores in the family home. He put a note out for the milkman: "No milk until Friday". He left a phone message for the school bus driver to say that his daughter Bethan would not be at school for the rest of the week. At around midday he sent a text on the phone of his wife, Catherine, to her friend Debbie cancelling their plan to attend a parent-teacher association meeting that evening. It read, "My mother's ill, we'll speak tomorrow." He let the family dog, Brandy, and the cat out.

Downstairs in the detached house in Barry, just outside of Cardiff on the south coast of Wales, all looked normal for a middle-class home in which four children and two pets had the run of the place.

Upstairs was not normal. When Mochrie went upstairs it was to clean up the blood. During the night he had methodically bludgeoned to death all those closest to him – Catherine, his wife; sons James, aged 18, and Luke, 14; and daughters Sian, 16, and Bethan, 10.

He spent that Wednesday carefully getting everything just as he wanted it, wiping away blood on the walls, pulling up the duvets over the heads of James, Luke and Catherine, as if to comfort them. Rosary beads had been placed on each of the bedsteads, possibly put there by Mochrie, a Catholic. His other tasks – cancelling the milk, the school lift, his wife's appointment – were part of his intention to shut out the world, to keep his dismaying, monstrous crime strictly in-house, and delay discovery of it for as long as possible.

As it was getting dark, he had one last thing to tidy up. He gulped a concoction of paracetamol and poisons, put a plastic bag over his head and hanged himself with a flex cord from the loft hatch.

His desire to conceal all this for as long as possible succeeded. Britain's most shocking family annihilation of recent times was not discovered for 11 days.

Debbie Zeraschi was best mates with Catherine Mochrie, regarding her neighbour as a sister. They were similar in age – Debbie being 40, Catherine, 45 – and their children were all close in years. "They used to go to dance classes, keep fit, salsa classes, all this type of thing that friends tend to do," said former Detective Chief Inspector Paul Bethell. "Always kept in close contact. On the evening of the night of 11 July, Debbie dropped Catherine off outside the house as normal, having been to a salsa class and had the usual brief discussion.

They gave each other a hug as they always did and made arrangements to speak the next day. Catherine was in a good mood. She was happy, she was buoyant, as Debbie said."

The two women spoke or saw each other every day – but then Debbie heard nothing from her friend for well over a week, not since 11 July, the day before the cryptic "we'll speak tomorrow" text. Debbie called and texted her friend but received no reply. She had been curious to see how Catherine was – had her mother recovered? – but had been left hanging.

They all lived on the Highlight Estate, on the outskirts of Barry. Debbie's home was around the corner from the Mochrie's five-bedroomed house. She popped round several times during Catherine's absence. "It seemed very still," she would say later. "The house was always full of life, always vibrant, with people coming in and out. Now, it seemed abandoned."

Bafflement was turning into concern. Debbie's teenage children said James Mochrie had not turned up for a planned weekend break. No one could contact Sian on her mobile. On Sunday, 23 July, Debbie called again at the Mochries'. "I began to notice things – the smell and the flies," she said. "For some reason, I thought I would look in the garage. As soon as I saw the car, I knew. They did not put it in the garage. It was always in the drive."

With a friend's help, she placed a ladder by an upstairs window and climbed it. She could see Luke's bed; there was a shape under the covers. Debbie called the police.

"At 8:30 that night, officers attended and forced entry into the house," said Paul Bethell, who would become the lead investigator on this case. Downstairs was messy, as might be expected in a large family home – trainers and shoes everywhere, clothes on the banister, James's guitar against the living-room wall.

"But, of course, when officers climbed the stairs to the first floor, there was this horrific scene," Bethell said. "Catherine was lying in her bedroom. She was face down on the bed, her head had been tilted to one side and her arms were straight at the side as if she'd been put in that position, and the duvet was pulled over her, almost as if to bizarrely comfort her in some way. And clearly, she had suffered considerable head trauma.

"The children were found in identical circumstances, each in their bedrooms, lying in their beds, all still dressed in their nightclothes, face down, heads tilted to the side, arms at their sides, and again all had suffered head trauma – probably the most horrific scene that anyone can possibly imagine.

"Officers then discovered Robert himself on the landing of the house. He had opened the attic hatch, tied a rope to the beam. He placed a plastic bag over his head, and he'd hung himself. And the pathology and the post-mortem results revealed through toxicology that he had taken a quantity of slug pellets, weedkiller and paracetamol. So, when you add those three things together with the plastic bag and the hanging, there was no question whatsoever as to what the state of Robert's mind was at that time."

He left no note.

* * *

Robert and Catherine were the "perfect" couple. Everybody said so.

This "perfect" image was captured in a family portrait taken on the occasion of Catherine's graduation as a mature student. Parents and children are smartly dressed, relaxed and beaming at the camera. The image would be reprinted countless times following the murder-suicide.

Catherine had just finished her degree in philosophy and sociology at Cardiff University. Only the night before Debbie Zeraschi saw her for the last time on Tuesday 11 July, the two women had been driven by Robert to Cardiff for a graduation party. He later picked them up at Barry train station on their return. He was in good form, laughing and making jokes. Debbie said, "I remember my last words to him were, 'Rob, you're an angel.'"

This was two nights before the massacre.

Jan Casault became friendly with Catherine as they studied together as mature students. She said Catherine "doted" on her four children. She would be reported in the media later as saying, "No one can understand what has gone on there, they seemed like a perfectly normal family. I met her husband quite a few times. He seemed pleasant but a bit on the quiet side." Friends would remember how delighted Robert was that Catherine had got her degree – one of the proudest moments of his life, he had said.

A former business partner of Robert's, Roger Cruttenden, would say Mochrie "absolutely worshipped" the children. Mike Clinch, headteacher at St Richard Gwyn Catholic

School, said the Mochries were very supportive of the school and Catherine was secretary of the parent-teacher association. "Both parents always came together to parents' evenings. Robert was softly spoken but always asked the questions you would expect from a caring parent. They were a very strong Catholic family. There was never any hint of anything sinister behind the scenes. The children were genuinely nice kids from a very normal, caring family."

The headteacher also paid tribute to the children. "Sian was quiet but very conscientious. She had just done her GCSEs and was expected to do very well. Luke was also doing well at school. It is a body blow. We are a very close community and it hurts. You just cannot comprehend what circumstances have led to this."

Three of Sian's friends, all aged 16, paid a tearful visit to the Mochrie house. One of them, Rachel, told a reporter that Sian was "a lovely girl who was always up for a laugh with her friends". Claire echoed what many people were saying: "They were a really nice family and they all seemed to get on really well. They were just a normal, ordinary family. They were very close."

Superintendent Colin Jones, the Divisional Commander, summed up the sense of shock at the scene inside number 43. "Our feelings are those of utter disbelief," he said. "It defies logic. It is not very often that you come across a house where there are six bodies."

Former chief inspector Paul Bethell emphasised how important religion was to the Mochries. "They were a staunch

Catholic family. Catherine regularly attended the Catholic church in Barry with the children."

Like many long-term couples, Catherine and Robert were not affectionate in public, but were seen as mutually supportive. Catherine may have shouldered most of the household tasks, but they would often share school runs and cooking duties. The tumult of work, school and family were constant, but Debbie's impression was that "they loved each other, they loved their children".

Bethell revealed some of the detail that the police uncovered about the family dynamic: "Robert Mochrie was 49 years of age and had been married for 23 years to Catherine. They lived in a detached house in Rutland Close in Barry, quite an affluent housing estate at the time. The property was valued in the early 90s in the region of £250,000.

"James had been successful at school and won a place at Bristol University to study law. Sian had just undertaken her GCSEs and had great success. Luke was the second son. Sadly, when he was eight years old, he suffered a brain tumour, which left him with some learning difficulties, problems with his speech. But what we were told was that he was a huge football fan, particularly Manchester United, and he loved his snooker. Friends have told us that often they would see Robert and Luke sitting together on the sofa at home, watching the football and snooker, which was one of their favourite pastimes.

"Bethan, the youngest, was autistic. She was described by family and friends as a little ray of sunshine. She was the one that brightened the house up, and the neighbours all spoke highly of the family and in particular all remembered Bethan out in the day walking around the estate, taking the family dog, Brandy, smiling and singing and saying hello."

They also lived in a safe environment. You rarely saw a police officer on the Highlight Estate. It was the epitome of comfortable suburbia. The modern architecture may have been uninspiring, but with its trim lawns, cul-de-sacs, young professionals and brick driveways, it was a secure and friendly environment in which to raise a family. It even kept its distance from the bright lights and tourist attractions of Barry Island itself, which was a 15-minute walk away. Barry, the largest coal-export port in the world by the early 20th century, had long since transformed itself into a leisure resort, with a pleasure park and beach. A local authority brochure cheerfully summed the town up like this: "There are few places in the world that combine coal and candyfloss, ships and chips, bananas and bumper-cars so seamlessly." For the Mochries, this town of around 60,000 people would have been an ideal family setting.

"Rutland Close is on an estate just off the coast," Paul Bethell said. "Barry Island itself is a very well-known area in South Wales, visited by thousands of people, particularly in summertime. Very popular with its seaside attractions, its small beach. But it is very much a seaside community. The children would have spent a great deal of time down on the seafront, as you would if you lived in the Barry area. It's an attractive place to live."

Catherine, who happened to be the sister of former Welsh rugby international and British Lion Terry Holmes, was more outgoing than Robert. She had her salsa classes, friends such as Debbie, and had just completed her studies in Cardiff. Robert, a quiet man, did not have many male friends, his socialising consisting of the odd pint down the pub, watching an occasional rugby match. "Robert was a good friend, a good man, a loving father and a good husband," Debbie said. "Rob was one of the least aggressive men I have ever known. He was quiet, not the most sociable of people. Telephone conversations were impossible – long silences, that sort of thing. That was Rob."

Police initially found many testimonies to the family's ordinariness and decency. Paul Bethell summed it up: "Robert had been a civil servant. He's described as an extremely loving and caring father and husband, a gentleman. There was certainly no indication whatsoever of any violence towards anyone, and he was particularly loving towards his children and Catherine. She was a highly intelligent woman. She was described as cheery and happy, Robert as more inward, not the best company in the world, if you like. He was quite an introverted character. A friend of the family told us that having a conversation with Robert was like pulling teeth. He was a quiet man who would sit in a corner on his own. But they stressed that he was gentle and calm."

Robert came from Falkirk originally, but spent most of his life in Wales. He had held a senior job at the Welsh Office, before leaving to run a couple of businesses. Catherine had also been a civil servant, which is how they met more than two decades previously, and went on to create a bustling life with their children.

Neighbour Maggie Richards was as in the dark about what had happened as everyone else who had known the Mochries. She said, "We hadn't seen them around, but we thought they had gone away on holiday. They were fine and didn't appear to have any problems."

And family friend Chris Williams was another who was dismayed by the ghastly turn of events at number 43. She said, "We are all at a loss. Robert was the guy who wouldn't hurt a fly."

Everyone thought the Mochries were a picture of suburban normality and happiness. Everyone was wrong.

"At the commencement of this investigation we were told Robert and his family were an ordinary family," said retired detective Paul Bethell. "However, nothing could be further from the truth."

Police found that Robert had a history of depression. In 1990 his doctor had referred him to a psychiatrist, Dr Brian Harris, because he felt so down and apparently had suicidal thoughts. In one telling phrase, he told Dr Harris his problems at work made him feel as if "someone had blown his head open with a shotgun". He was prescribed medications but would not be admitted to a psychiatric ward for further treatment.

PAUL BETHELL,
RETIRED DETECTIVE
CHIEF INSPECTOR

Robert did not tell anyone, not even his wife, Catherine, about his feelings of futility.

"In 1993, he again visited the psychiatrist and again repeated what he had said previously," Bethell said. "But with the addition that he'd suffered weight loss, he was suffering with fatigue and depression, and that on this occasion he had become delusional. And he talked about a ball of light on his shoulder and someone standing behind him." Again, he declined any further help or for anyone else to be informed. So, rather than accept care and support from those closest to him, such as Catherine, Robert kept his despair to himself. Dr Harris would say later, "With a crisis such as debt or divorce, most of us would find some way of coping. But to those prone to delusions, their belief system could grow until they believed that the only way out was for everyone to die."

As setbacks and stress mounted in the years to come, Robert's reluctance to open up about his vulnerabilities cannot have helped him. Bethell said, "Mental health is talked about openly now, thankfully, and discussed – there is support there for people, and individuals are aware of the issues that perhaps family and friends have. But we're going back 20, 21 years here, when things were a little different in relation to mental health. People were far more reluctant to discuss their problems. Robert kept it a secret, he didn't want anybody to know, probably through shame or a feeling of being a failure."

One family issue he could share with his wife was the health of his children. They would have had ongoing concerns about Luke, whose life-threatening brain tumour had left him with learning difficulties. Meanwhile, to help Bethan with her autism, she was sent to a special school. This, Paul Bethell suggests, added a further financial draw on the family income. Criminal psychologist Dr David Holmes believes that while both parents were devoted to their children, Robert may have been more protective than he needed to be. He may have left the security of the civil service because of the stress he was feeling, but another reason may have been a desire to spend more time with Bethan.

Sex and money, however, were the two major breakdowns that were secretly festering between Robert and Catherine.

Robert had huge debts, which, like his depression, he kept hidden. After leaving the civil service, he and some partners bought a dilapidated hotel in 1994. They renovated it and refashioned it into a nightclub, the Power Station. This seaside venue pulled in quite a crowd from Cardiff and made a profit. Three years later, Robert got out of the nightclub business and poured his profit into a 22-bedroom hotel in Haverfordwest. The Pembroke House Hotel, however, was a disaster. This large hotel in a rural area never took off, and Robert's bid to replicate his success with the Power Station became a financial liability instead. In 1999 the hotel had to close after fire devastated the kitchens. There was also a dispute with the insurers, who refused to pay out to cover the losses. Robert's prospects slid further when his attempt to sell the property failed to even reach its reserve price of £150,000. From this point, Robert was losing money, with £126,000 gushing from his business account in the period up to his death. The Mochries were £200,000 in debt at the time Robert destroyed his family. Whatever Catherine knew of the scale of the family's indebtedness, she did not share with her friend Debbie Zeraschi.

"The bank had recently called in an £80,000 loan," former detective Bethell said. "Bailiffs visited the house in relation to a £5,000 debt. Now, apparently there had been some minor argument between Catherine and Robert, which friends became aware of. It was believed that Catherine may not have known the actual enormity of the financial problems Robert had, although obviously she became aware that there were issues."

The arrival of bailiffs on the doorstep, in addition to causing friction between Robert and Catherine, might have punctured Robert's self-esteem as head of the family and chief provider. Such a public revelation of his problems would have rocked his desperate attempts to project an image that all was well.

Catherine had secrets too. David Osborne had been a long-time friend of the family. He would look after the family house when they went on holiday. He later took up the job as hotel manager for Robert. At some point, he and Catherine began a brief sexual relationship. Osborne would later tell the inquest in Cardiff that it occurred five months before the murders. "I saw her once after that, soon after her birthday," Osborne said. "She seemed all right, but we had a slight argument." When asked whether Robert Mochrie had known of the relationship, Osborne replied, "He never indicated that he knew about the relationship."

No evidence was found that Catherine was planning to leave Robert, but she was clearly dissatisfied in the marriage. She had another relationship after Osborne, this time with a man she knew from the pub, Paul Wyatt. She would meet him for coffee on the Monday before her murder. She even sent him a message just after midnight on the night of her death – "Couldn't call. Battery dead. Call later." It is impossible to know if she might have wanted this to develop into something serious. "Certainly, there were two brief affairs, so the marriage clearly wasn't a happy one in that respect," Bethell said.

There were further revelations about this labyrinth of hidden unhappiness and secrets. Again, Paul Bethell revealed what the investigation uncovered: "We discovered that Robert was meeting a sex worker twice weekly. He would meet her in a vehicle and indulge in sexual activities for which he paid. The sex worker, in fact, told the investigating officers that he allegedly said that his marriage was over. There was no suggestion, however, that either Catherine or Robert intended to leave each other or end the marriage. But, certainly, both partners were unhappy in respect of their sexual life and their closeness."

Charmaine Jacobs contacted Bethell's team after the bodies were found to say that Robert had been her regular client for two years. Every week on a Tuesday, and sometimes Thursday, he would drive his wife's Renault Clio to Charmaine's patch in Penarth Road, Cardiff, and then take her to an industrial estate. There she would masturbate him for £50. Afterwards, he would talk to her about his hotel, his family. "He talked about his marriage, saying there were problems – he said he was not having sex any more," she said. Each rendez-vous would last around 20 minutes.

He saw Charmaine on the evening of Tuesday 11 July, just hours before he murdered his wife and children. "It was pissing down with rain…" Charmaine said. "He was quiet that night."

"The house had turned from a family home into an unimaginable house of horrors," said former Detective Chief Inspector Paul Bethell.

Mochrie waited until the family were asleep. He then moved from bedroom to bedroom and beat each child and his wife to death. Son James, who was nearly six feet tall, and even 14-year-old Luke, were taller and more powerfully built than five foot eight inch Robert, but there were no signs of a struggle, no defence wounds.

Blood on the headboards, walls, floors and furniture in each bedroom. Eighteen blows struck.

Robert's attacks must have been coldly efficient and relatively quiet. Bethell said, "It was not mayhem or a blood-bath. It's methodical. It's controlled, managed. He's used some degree of pre-planning. Picture the scene. The house is in darkness, silent, and he is walking round. He goes from room to room. He strikes each of them with a blow or blows to the head. He then covers them with the duvet."

Apart from the unimaginable horror of it, Bethell was struck by unexplained aspects to Robert's behaviour. "A knife was found underneath James's bed. Now that knife showed traces of the blood from all the children. Unfortunately, because of the decomposition of the bodies – there'd been an 11-day period [before the family was found], the weather was warm, it was July – the pathologist was unable to say whether any of the children or Catherine had in fact been stabbed, although the weapon and the blood tends to suggest that, obviously. But, certainly, what did came to light was that all had suffered head trauma with what was described as a blunt instrument." Dental records had to be used to identify the family.

"It was never confirmed what Robert had used to kill the family," Bethell said, "although it was believed that a hammer, some sort of pickaxe, or a small ice pick might have been the murder weapon. Robert had also made an attempt to mop up, if you like, some of the bloodstain in Bethan's room by wiping the walls, which was quite bizarre behaviour because it was totally pointless. Clearly, his state of mind was deteriorating rapidly at that point. We believe that Robert was certainly alive for somewhere in the region of 24 hours after the death of Catherine and the children."

Criminal psychologist Dr David Holmes speculated about the mental state of an apparently caring father being able to carry out such an act. "Compounding the brutality of Robert Mochrie's choice of how he killed his children and his wife was the fact that he would have had to do these sequentially, one by one," he said. "The idea that you would beat someone that you love with a blunt instrument, we're not talking about a quick, easy death. We're talking about perhaps hitting two or three times. This is not something that you would repeat unless you had a certain element of callousness or determination.

"To repeatedly use a blunt instrument on one of your children, but then to progress to the next child and start that again and again and again... this takes quite a lot of either extreme determination or barely repressed rage."

Dr Holmes saw the seeds of Robert's crime in his depression. "Robert Mochrie had serious financial problems, he had deep marital problems. Possibly all of these could have been resolved. However, when disorder kicks in, depressive individuals cannot see the light at the end of the tunnel. Everything is awful. Everything is closing in on them. It was a cul-de-sac he was walking into, and he had no other option than to actually get rid of himself. He decided that rather than face ruin, the family should also join him in his suicide bid. In other words, he was kind of saving them from a more awful reality by killing them."

Was there not also an element of selfishness and control in Robert's methodical destruction of his family? He may have

been facing ruin, the emotional bond with Catherine was spiritless and stale, Luke and Bethan's health needs were ongoing, but this final episode for them all would be the one thing of which the depressed and flailing Robert could be master. So, he could indulge in gestures such as covering his victims with the bedclothes

DR DAVID
HOLMES, CRIMINAL
PSYCHOLOGIST

and the cleaning up of Bethan's blood. As Bethell described it, the latter was "totally pointless' in that Robert knew there was no way this massacre could be covered up, there could be no washing away of guilt. Instead, these were his perverse acts of contrition – I had to beat you to death, but look how I love and care for you. The cancelling of the milk and the other ploys to prevent the crime being uncovered for as long as possible seem like a further attempt to exercise control and ensure there could be no outside interference. This was Robert's family, and he would do what he thought necessary.

Criminal psychologist Gareth Norris offered a further insight into Robert's apparently strange conduct. "There was evidence that he tried to clean up some of the blood. Now obviously he was not going to get away with this, it's not like he was trying to cover his tracks. He wants to try to make it look as clean and calculated as a killing could be, in an almost merciful way. Cleaning up the blood is almost him trying to cover up the level of violence on display here.

"At the ends of the beds police were to find rosary beads for each of the children after he's killed them. We can't be sure if he's done this because he really believes they're going on to an afterlife or whether it's a kind of gesture, that he's trying to be respectful for what he's done to his children."

Having spent almost 24 hours alone in the house getting everything as he wanted it, he committed suicide. "When he does actually decide to kill himself," Norris said, "Robert takes an overdose of tablets, some poison, he puts a plastic bag on his head, and then he also hangs himself. So there is a high level of what we might call overkill there, in that he wants to make sure that he's gone, he doesn't want to be left to face the music. This was not a suicide that was a cry for help. This was him wanting to kill himself." His final act of authority.

Detective Superintendent Kevin O'Neill described the scene. He said, "It was by all accounts a dreadful scene and we are offering counselling to officers."

Forensic expert Diane Ivory described what a difficult task this would have been for the officers. "When a murder's taken place and a body's not been found for some while, there will be quite heavy decomposition, and that's what happened in this case. So it was quite difficult to establish what the attack had been. The recovery of these bodies must have been horrendous. Each one has to be preserved in such a way as to get as much evidence from them as possible, bearing in mind the state of decomposition. It would have been just horrendous to do. I know as scene examiners we all have to do it, but to have to deal with so many bodies in one place is terribly distressing.

"This kind of crime scene is one that would haunt you for a very long time. With a scene like this after so many days, it's not just the sight that you're faced with, it's also the smells. You go home, you try to forget. I always say I've got lots of little boxes in my head with the lids tightly shut, but every now and again the lids pop open, it's always there. You just try to do the job you need to do on the day, the best you can, for whoever it is that's been murdered."

Robert Mochrie committed a rare crime known as familicide – killing several members of his own family (as opposed to filicide: the murder of your own children). He was also what criminologists call a "family annihilator".

The term seems to have been coined by Professor P E Dietz in 1986. He described the family annihilator as "usually the senior man of the house, who is depressed, paranoid, intoxicated or a combination of these". This type of man – and it is overwhelmingly men who do this – might kill himself after murdering his family, or force the police to kill him. Two other professors refined the category further. James Alan Fox and Jack Levin described these killers as having "a long history of frustration and failure, through childhood and into adult life. He has tremendous difficulty both at home and at work in achieving happiness and success. Over time, repeated frustration can erode a person's ability to cope, so much so that even modest disappointments seem catastrophic."

This type has a warped sense of love and believes he is saving his loved ones from misery and hardship. While this category of murder bears parallels with revenge killers, who murder their children to cause pain to their partners, it is a distinct crime. What has been termed the "altruistic" family killer has a monstrous self-obsession and can barely see his children as separate entities. In his twisted world view, when his life ends, theirs must too.

A team from Birmingham University – Professor Elizabeth Yardley, Professor David Wilson and Dr Adam Lynes – studied family annihilators in Britain from 1980 to

2012. Their search suggested that cases of family annihilation were rising, with the figure going from six cases reported in the press in the 1980s, to 18 in the 1990s, and a further increase between 2000 and 2009, when there were 28 cases.

Almost 60 per cent of the killings were committed at home, most often by stabbing. The range of occupations of the men responsible was broad: surgeon, doctor, accountant, librarian, driving instructor, marketing executive, painter and decorator, and businessman.

The primary motivations for murder were threat of family break-up and bankruptcy. The next biggest explanations were honour killing (the father feeling shamed by his family) and mental illness.

The Birmingham academics formulated four categories of family annihilator: self-righteous (or revenge); disappointed (family has let him down); anomic (father has failed via redundancy or bankruptcy, for example); paranoid (an external threat from, say, social services, will destroy his family).

Robert Mochrie, who featured in the data for the Birmingham study, clearly falls into the anomic band (the term refers to the idea that individuals experience instability from either a breakdown in standards/values or a lack of purpose/ideals). A strong feature of this definition is how the man's family is a badge of economic success. Robert certainly looked like a businessman who was winning. He had the detached house, the car, the teenagers' bedrooms stocked with televisions and CD players. But as we have seen, this was an illusion. He was heading towards bankruptcy. Was he dreading the ignominy of having all this taken away? The failure of their way of life would be down to him.

"What seems to link each of the subcategories that we have identified," the Birmingham academics concluded, "is masculinity and the need to exert power and control in situations when the annihilator feels that his masculinity has, in some way, been threatened. For these men, the family role of the father was fundamental to their masculine identities and, prior to the murders, the family had, to some extent, ceased to perform its masculinity-affirming functions for them."

Criminal psychologist Gareth Norris also saw the crisis building for Robert with his realisation that his mounting problems would be impossible to hide much longer. He said, "Sometimes these cracks that appear – very often most people don't see them, or people hide them, and it's not until some time later that we discover the truth behind the family. This idea of the perfect family doesn't really exist. It's something that we perhaps all aspire to.

"It was all about to come out into the open [for the Mochries], and this was the thing that caused him [Robert] to snap. This wouldn't have been a decision he made overnight. It would have been something he considered for some time. He really couldn't face this public humiliation."

Criminal psychologist Dr David Holmes said Robert's careful management of the crime indicated no desire to leave a message or explain what he had done. "I don't think Robert Mochrie would have intended to leave a note. I think, to be honest, that he hoped that the debts and the marital discord would be buried with his family and himself. He did not want to explain the awfulness of what he felt and saw in his own life."

Dr Holmes also wondered if Robert had in fact discovered that Catherine had seen other men, and what effect that might have had. "That may have put another element into his mind, that of, if you like, the selfish gene, the idea that if these affairs have been taking place, maybe his children weren't his, maybe of his being fooled all his life. Maybe this contains a small element of jealous rage buried within it.

"To actually think in terms of killing your children, your wife, in order to save them from a worse reality, perhaps could be seen as someone who is overly caring, who pushes it far beyond the limits. However, he didn't poison them, he didn't stand at a distance and pull a trigger. He beat them to death, including the handicapped child he cared for so much. To place yourself into that situation, it would be difficult to still maintain the view of someone who is sensitive and caring. This would seem to be an act of some repressed violence. A depressive person may have just dropped the blunt instrument and couldn't do it at the last minute."

Former head of the investigation Paul Bethell summed up Robert Mochrie's point of no return: "You have the financial issue, the problems with the daughter, Bethan, the difficulties that Luke was having with his health, and then Robert with his mental health, the infidelity of Catherine and Robert. You put all these things together and you could imagine the pressure he described at one point as feeling like his head had been blown apart. And you can imagine all these issues gathering pace, gathering pace in his mind."

It is hard not to wonder if Robert also feared Catherine's burgeoning independence. She had just got a university degree, she had friends, interests. It is ironic that reticent Robert, who wanted to conceal his mental health problems, turned to Charmaine Jacobs for conversation in addition to commercial sex. As he plunged into his somewhat self-imposed despair of feeling like a failure, he may have sensed that Catherine may soon no longer need him. Or perhaps he feared the emasculating prospect of her going to work and taking over his role as chief provider for the family. Somewhere in his thinking may have been a suspicion that one day Catherine and the children may not rely on him at all.

Since the tragedy on Rutland Close, Barry has gone on to enjoy fame as the setting for the hit BBC sitcom *Gavin & Stacey*, and has been tipped as one of the best places to buy a house in Wales. The waterfront has seen considerable redevelopment, old properties have been repurposed as modern private flats, and there is plenty to do outdoors, from Whitmore Bay Beach to Porthkerry Country Park, from a summer music festival – none other than GlastonBarry – to the Barry War Museum.

While the town may have become an attractive option for new arrivals put off by Cardiff's property prices, longstanding residents have not forgotten the shock and pain Robert Mochrie's crime left in Barry. Ex-detective Paul Bethell said,

"I think that today, even 20 years on, there's very few, if any, people who would have forgotten the family, the tragedy and the circumstances. And it's probably something, sadly, like many infamous cases, that will remain with that community for years and years to come. How do you forget it? How do you get over it?

"You must try and get on with your lives. But, yes, certainly it's something that would be whispered about and people would remember the family and the sadness of it all. You know, this wonderful family, this lovely family… what a dreadful, dreadful way for everything to end."

The outpouring of shock and grief began at the funeral. More than 400 friends, family and neighbours attended at St Helen's Church in Barry. Among them was Catherine Mochrie's brother, the former rugby star Terry Holmes. Schoolfriends of the Mochrie children hugged each other during the service. The family had decided that Catherine and the children would be buried together. Robert was cremated at a separate location.

Debbie Zeraschi, Catherine's good friend, told the congregation, "There doesn't seem to be any words to explain the beauty of Cath. She was a peace-maker who hated arguing. She had very strong principles and always fought for the right cause."

The Mochries had been regular churchgoers, which might explain the presence of 11 priests at the service. The scene as five coffins were carried into the church must have been heartbreaking.

Parish priest Father Patrick O'Gorman said, "Sometimes life confronts us with things we cannot explain. Tonight we stand before the inexplicable – tender, raw and to some degree broken – unable to adequately put into words what we would like to express."

At a police press conference, a statement by Terry Holmes was read out: "Our family have been completely devastated by the loss of my sister and her family. I simply do not know how to begin putting into words how we are feeling. We are supporting each other as best we can through this terrible time."

Catherine and the children are buried in Western Cemetery, in Ely, Cardiff. The gravestone reads that Catherine and "her beloved children" were taken on 23 July 2000. "May they all rest in peace."

Robert Mochrie conformed in most respects to the definition of a family annihilator. He was white, middle class, a good father, a conscientious provider. He had no convictions. He was, in effect, a model citizen.

The maze of crises he faced – financial, marital, his children's health, his depression – would torment most of us. However, the scale and nature of these problems do not explain or rationalise his grotesque solution for them.

Dr Chris Milroy, a forensic pathologist at the University of Sheffield's medico-legal centre, when being interviewed by a newspaper about this case, said, "Is it just a series of factors – his wife cheating on him, depression, being bad with his finances? [Robert Mochrie] certainly had more problems than most. The real question is, why aren't there more Robert Mochries? These are not uncommon human problems."

It is extremely difficult to untangle the thought processes of a man such as Robert Mochrie, who ended up stealthily moving through his house in the dark, believing that bludgeoning his wife and children to death was an act of love. He tried to minimise their pain, so that they probably had no idea what hit them.

He was loving, concerned. And terrifying.

One plaintive question hangs in the air. Paul Bethell, whose painstaking investigation revealed the sad truth of the "perfect family" at 43 Rutland Close, summed it up in a throwaway comment. "If he'd had further support, if he had made people aware of his problems, people that could have helped, perhaps this whole issue could have been avoided."

PIERRE LEGRIS

Bournemouth

5

"A bad man and a very, very poor liar"

Bournemouth, 2014
Victim: Rui Li
Murderer: Pierre Legris

"It was 27 May 2014. I was a station desk officer on duty at Bournemouth Police Station. A guy comes into the inquiry office, that was Pierre Legris. He says to me that he's been away for three days, driving up and down the country, he's returned home and his wife's not there. Her daughter is at home, but she hasn't seen her for two days either. So I said, 'Well, OK, we'll take some details.'"

This was Steve Coward recalling an encounter with a member of the public at 7.40 am. Steve was not a police officer – the role of desk officer having evolved into a civilian job – but he had dealt with plenty of people reporting crimes and knew when there was something off-kilter about them.

"I took his name and address and [his wife] Rui Li's name, date of birth. I asked various questions. Was this out of character? Was she vulnerable in any way? Was she on any medication that she needed? I took the details and put them on the computer."

Legris told Coward that they had another property in Bournemouth, apart from their home address, and that he had been to that address looking for Rui Li. He said that her mobile phone was on charge there, but she wasn't there. He had then spent the night there, sleeping and awaiting her return, but she was still absent.

"When he first spoke to me," Coward continued, "Pierre Legris described Rui Li as his wife. But later in the conversation, he referred to her as his girlfriend. I've been married twice, I've been divorced twice, and every time I knew who my wife was. I never once considered her to be my girlfriend. And I stopped him and said, 'Look, you know, I'm sending this information to other people, I don't want to mislead anybody. So, is she your wife or your girlfriend?' He became very vague and refused to answer, even when I pressed him on it. So, I left it. But that was the first moment I thought that something might not be quite right here."

Legris said that his wife, a Chinese national, was a nurse at Poole Hospital. He then said she might have gone back to China. He said he had made inquiries with her home country and was awaiting an email reply.

"I said we're treating her as a missing person and are concerned for her welfare," Coward recalled. "Then he said to me that she was actually supposed to be on duty at Poole Hospital that very morning, at 7.30. I said, 'Have you phoned the hospital?' He said, 'What for?'"

STEVE COWARD, RETIRED STATION DESK OFFICER, DORSET POLICE

Coward pointed out the obvious – that she might be at work. So, the desk officer phoned the hospital several times, but could only get an answer machine. On the fifth occasion he gave the receiver to Legris and told him to leave a message that he was concerned for Rui Li and to ask for confirmation of whether she was at work or not.

"Then he made an excuse to go out of the police station and make a telephone call," Coward said. "I carried on putting the details in, when he came back in and I said, 'What's the news?' He said he had a message back from the hospital saying she's not there. So I said, 'Are you going to the hospital now?' And he said, 'Well, what for?'"

The desk officer pointed out that Poole Hospital was a big establishment and his wife might have been moved or seconded to a different ward. Legris said that he still would not go to the hospital. "He said, 'I've got to go to work.'"

Again, Coward made plain the obvious, that a police officer would need to follow up and speak to him about his missing wife. Legris did not want to stick around and said he had to get to work.

"So I said, 'If you go to work, perhaps we can phone you and make an appointment to come round and see you, but you are going to have to be spoken to.' Legris said, 'Well, it's very, very noisy at my work and I might not hear the phone,' and I'm like, OK. He refused to stay, and he went. As soon as he left the inquiry office I thought, if this guy really cared about his wife he'd have been down to the hospital half an hour before she was due to be at work, waiting for her car to arrive, and said something like, 'Darling, where have you been? I've been worried about you.' He didn't do that. And when I said to him, we're going to have to phone you and a police officer is going to be investigating the whereabouts of your wife, I thought he would have said, 'I'll keep the phone on vibrate and it'll be by my ear.' But he did nothing like that."

Coward had dealt with plenty of members of the public reporting missing friends or loved ones. They were nearly always agitated, anxious, and often tearful or emotional. Some brought a friend or relative for support. "Pierre Legris was the polar opposite," Coward said. "He showed absolutely no emotion whatsoever. I thought to myself, this guy is just coming in to tick the box to say that he's reported somebody missing."

He called his sergeant and said a guy had just come in to report his wife missing, but he was not at all distressed and gave all the wrong answers.

"I said I think you better look at this one really, really hard. The sergeant read what I'd written on the report, then contacted the inspector and said, 'I agree, this is weird, can you have a look at it, sir?'

"A few minutes later, an inspector came into the inquiry office. I knew him well, offered him a cup of tea. I told him the story. By the afternoon, a few people started turning up in the inquiry office that you wouldn't ordinarily see there, plainclothes guys with lanyards saying that they worked for Dorset Police. I recognised one of them and said, 'Are you here for the nurse?'

"I said, 'Tell them to come and see me. He's done her in, I know he has.'"

Bournemouth is on the Dorset coast. Like Blackpool, it developed as a holiday resort during the Victorian era, originally being marketed as a health resort. In the middle of the 19th century it was still a village with a population in the hundreds. It became a town in 1870, the same year the railway arrived, delivering an increase in visitors. The Winter Gardens and Pleasure Gardens were developed, and the Bournemouth Arcade was built in that decade. The population had ballooned to 37,000 by 1891. Unlike Blackpool, Bournemouth is a rather staid, conservative town. Today, there are around 200,000 people living there, and while tourism is important to the local economy, Bournemouth is also something of a business hub for the region, with companies such as JP Morgan and Nationwide having bases there.

To all appearances, Pierre Legris, aged 61, was a sober, respectable local figure. He had an interest in his family's second-hand car business and garage, as well as some property. Wife Rui Li was liked by her colleagues at Poole Hospital. The couple had married in 2007, both having been married previously. Rui Li had an 18-year-old daughter, Lu Yao, from her first marriage. Legris's son from his earlier marriage, Jonathan, aged 27, worked in the family's car business and had been an aspiring racing driver and contemporary of future Formula 1 champion Lewis Hamilton.

Rui Li, who was 44 when she disappeared, had moved to the United Kingdom in 2003. She came from a prosperous family in China, which might explain her flamboyant choice of car, a Porsche Boxster with personalised number plate. The first of many questions thrown up by this case was how much she really knew about the man she had married.

A French national, Legris had in the past used another name, Alain Baron. He was also a bigamist. When he married Rui Li, he was actually still married to his first wife, Irene Smith, aged 66. She lived in the Bournemouth suburb of Boscombe, on St Clement's Road, near the car business, Cromer Motors.

Legris and Li's personal life had an unconventional side. They lived on Burnham Drive in Bournemouth and had a second property on Wolverton Road, from where they ran a massage service. This was advertised on Gumtree, and sexual services were sometimes provided by Li, with Legris present and sometimes participating. Legris would later try to use this sideline as an explanation for what happened to Li.

Strains began to affect the relationship. Li told Legris she was planning to adopt a child from China. It is possible that the prospect of such a change in lifestyle might have been opposed by Legris, a rather manipulative character. He was a man who habitually used his second "wife" in various sexual transactions in pursuit of money or leisure. He may have recoiled from the idea of parenting with her. A child would also be an expense that Legris, whose finances were in a desperate tangle, could certainly do without.

Legris's legal wife, Irene Smith, was in danger of losing her home because she owed money on it. A mortgage was not an option for her because of her age. She and Legris had planned for him to buy the property and she had transferred £50,000 to his account for a deposit. One issue for them was that the bank was asking questions about this money, but another was that Legris owed £20,000 to Li's relatives in China. He could use some of Irene Smith's deposit money to pay this off, but the animosity between the two women would have made such a move a cause of huge friction for Legris.

It is hard not to suspect that the whole point of the bigamist's "marriage" to Li was to siphon money from her. She worked as a nurse, participated in the massage sideline, and had a wealthy family. Her desire to raise another child may have indicated to Legris that her ability, or willingness, to be such an earner would come to an end. If he had also exhausted all the goodwill of her family to bail him out, he may have been facing severe financial problems. The answer to these, it would later be argued, lay in getting his hands on her life insurance policy. This was worth £300,000. In addition, she owned the Wolverton Road property, which she hoped to sell to realise a profit of £100,000.

"I don't think it was a deep, meaningful emotional relationship," said criminal psychologist Dr David Holmes. "He was controlling, had little emotion, a greedy man."

On Friday, 23 May 2014, the start of the Spring Bank Holiday weekend, Li was recorded on the Poole Hospital CCTV leaving work in her Porsche. The following week, colleagues from the hospital started to make inquiries about her subsequent absence. Her daughter also asked questions about her whereabouts. And Pierre Legris turned up the following Tuesday at Bournemouth police station to report her missing.

Some six years later, station desk officer Steve Coward was still bemused by how unconvincing Legris was in the role of concerned husband. "To be perfectly honest, I was insulted by the fact that he thought he could get such a bad story past me," he said. "It wasn't that I was good or an expert or anything. He wouldn't have got it past anybody. It was such a bad story. He was a bad liar and he made lots of mistakes, even just while chatting to me. I just did my bit and I left all the difficult stuff to other people."

The other people included Dorset Police sergeant Paul Vacher, who was the senior house-to-house co-ordinator for the Major Crime Investigation Team. "At that time in mid-May," he said, "it was understood that a gentleman had walked into Bournemouth police station and reported his wife, Rui Li, a Chinese lady, as missing. The inquiries officer who took that information was not entirely satisfied with the explanation that was given. And as a consequence, things swung into action and after a few days I was called and asked to conduct house-to-house inquiries in the residential street where they both lived. I think I had a team of six, seven or eight officers and we began to conduct house-to-house inquiries in that street in Queens Park." Though these inquiries were extensive, no one had seen Rui Li for several days.

"When a person goes missing it's not always the case that they leave a trace behind," said Vacher, "but usually there's something for the inquiry team to go on. Obviously, worst case scenario, people leave suicide notes, otherwise they're seen driving away. But on occasions like Rui Li, there was really no trace of her from the outset. That is unusual. And, of course, the house-to-house inquiries that we were doing didn't give any clue as to where she had gone. There was a suggestion that she may have returned to China, but no doubt inquiries will have been made at borders. And, of course, if she hadn't exited the country, that was another reason for concern. That was all added to the inquiry office's initial misgivings when Pierre Legris walked into the police station. That's why it got ramped up quite quickly."

Finally, during questioning, it was Pierre Legris's son, Jonathan, who gave the police their breakthrough. Later in court it would be revealed by his barrister that Jonathan broke down in tears, revealing that he had left a Fiat Punto he owned in the Southbourne area of Bournemouth on his father's instructions. While Jonathan might move cars around for his father as part of the garage business, leaving them in several locations, this appeared to be a journey with a difference.

Paul Vacher recalled: "I bumped into a detective colleague. He told me that inquiries were progressing quite fast and that it was expected that Rui Li's body might be found imminently in the boot of a car. He jumped into my car and we were instructed to drive to an address in Southbourne, where we found a car – if I remember correctly, a Jaguar – and we were instructed to open the boot of the car on the driveway. We did so, and there was nothing untoward in it. We were then told to stand by for a few minutes as further information was being gleaned from the interview team. I believe they were interviewing Jonathan Legris at the time.

"A few minutes later, we were asked to search for a Fiat Punto. It wasn't known where it was parked, but we had been given a registration number. We drove around that area frantically trying to find this Fiat Punto, and probably after 30 minutes or so, we found it parked in a residential street [Verwood Crescent], locked and unattended in the dark. We stepped forward to open the boot when the command came through that we shouldn't do so until forensic officers arrived. So we waited. A forensic officer arrived five minutes later. He suited himself up with all the forensic kit and we opened the boot of the car. Unfortunately, it was correct. A female body was wrapped up in plastic in the boot of that car.

"I've had many years' police service. It's not the first time I've seen bodies in those circumstances, but every one is a very sad thing to see, a life snatched away so violently. It was a dark and lonely scene. It was clear what was wrapped in the plastic. Obviously, we weren't going to unwrap the plastic there and then, but there was an odour, an odour that is associated with death, the odour that lives with you, that you recognise immediately."

Verwood Crescent was a long residential street, predominantly bungalows, an area popular with retirees. Virtually none of the properties had CCTV cameras – apart from one where

Jonathan Legris had left his Punto. The police were delighted by their good luck. The video recording confirmed that Legris Junior had parked the Punto, locked it and walked away.

Pierre Legris was also being questioned – and he was changing his story. Having first denied knowing anything about the death of Li, he then said he had returned to find that she had been murdered. He had panicked, he claimed, wrapped her in a building sheet and placed her in his Ford Transit van. His reason for attempting to cover up this horrific discovery was that he feared that their adventurous sex life would be made public (it would later be stated in court that Legris and Rui Li were involved in local wife-swapping networks). It would also later become part of his defence that he suspected a disgruntled customer of their massage service may have followed Li home and murdered her.

Rui Li's body was found in the car on 30 May 2014. A post-mortem revealed she had received several blows to the back of the head with a heavy object, with one particularly forceful strike penetrating deeply. She would have bled considerably. When Legris wrapped her in the sheeting she would have still been alive. Police were unable to find the blunt object used to murder Li, and there was not very much blood at the crime scene, the couple's home on Burnham Drive. It was clear that the killer had made a considerable effort to eradicate any clues with a thorough clean-up.

The attack took place on 23 May after Li left work. The house was having extensive building work done to it, and

Legris had bought several bags of cement. Police would come to suspect that he may have planned to bury the body somehow in the building work, but his scheme for disposing of it would remain unclear. The day after the murder, Legris and his son drove the Transit van with the body in it to the family's garage, which was owned by Irene Smith and run by Pierre and Jonathan. There, his son changed the van's starter motor while his stepmother's body was still inside.

Over the holiday weekend, Legris carried on as if nothing had happened. On Saturday, the day after the murder, he had taken Irene Smith to a dance competition in Watford. He was seen arm-in-arm with his first wife. On Sunday he ate lunch with his family. On Tuesday, having reported Li missing at Bournemouth police station, Legris moved her body to his son's Fiat Punto. Jonathan Legris then dumped the car in nearby Verwood Crescent, where it was found three days later.

Pierre Legris was eventually charged with murder and went on trial at Winchester Crown Court. Before the trial began, he pleaded guilty to bigamy and received a three-year sentence, which would run concurrently with the sentence he was later given for murder.

In court Legris was portrayed as a "controlling bigamist" who had murdered Rui Li to get his hands on her life insurance money to pay off his "desperate" debts. Nigel Lickley QC, prosecuting, said following the murder that Legris had been "cool and focused and clear in what he was doing". He also had "a plan and it involved others, his son, Jonathan Legris, and his other wife, Irene Smith".

Smith had provided a false alibi for Legris, going along with his claim that they had spent the evening of the murder together eating a meal and watching *EastEnders* at her home. However, CCTV footage showed him arriving there at about 4.45am. Smith also helped her husband by hiring a storage facility and putting some of his clothes and French passport there, presumably to facilitate any bid by him to flee the country.

The jury also saw CCTV video of father and son driving the Transit van with Li's body inside from the murder scene in Burnham Road to Cromer Motors, the family firm. The prosecutor said, "It was all planned and agreed the van would be moved back to the garage, they would carry on as normal and deal with Rui Li at some future time."

Pierre Legris was found guilty of murder on 27 February 2015 and sentenced to life, with a minimum term of 25 years. Jonathan received two years for assisting his father. Irene Smith was sentenced to three years for assisting an offender and perverting the course of justice. Wife and son were acquitted of conspiracy to murder.

The judge, Mr Justice Dingemans, said that as well as a financial motive, Pierre Legris might have murdered Li because of her decision to adopt a child. "It may equally have been the fact that Pierre Legris, as a controlling person, was not prepared to deal with the apparently late decision that Ms Li had made to adopt a child from China, which would have compromised his way of living."

The officer who headed the investigation, Detective Inspector Marcus Hester of Dorset Police's Major Crime

Investigation Team, said: "This was a detailed and complex investigation, which involved officers from across the force. Pierre Legris killed Rui Li out of greed, placed her body in the boot of a van, before driving to Watford to enjoy a weekend with his first wife, Irene Smith.

"He lied repeatedly to the police and went to great efforts to hide her body. I hope the sentences handed out today will bring some closure to Rui Li's daughter and her family in China."

Steve Coward, the station desk officer whose suspicions about Legris first raised the alarm about him, gave evidence during the trial. He recalled, "The thing that I got out of the case most was that you never really know how close you are to danger. She [Rui Li] didn't know, and look what happened to her. I was always a bit sad about that."

Or did Rui Li actually have her own suspicions about Pierre Legris? Her daughter, Lu Yao, told the trial that her mother had given her a will she had written. Li clearly did not want her husband to take anything he was not entitled to. Ms Lu also revealed that her mother told her that when she went on climbing trips with Legris she feared he would push her off the mountain. The dead woman had clearly been under no illusion about the danger Legris presented.

The trial and evidence leave the strong impression that Legris was a callous and manipulative user of people. Li was exploited and then brutally discarded when her usefulness to him subsided, and he saw there was one final payout to be got out of her.

However, events in court left many questions unanswered. How did Legris inveigle members of his family into his plot? The former police officer who had searched for Rui Li's body, Paul Vacher, said, "I think it's despicable. I can only imagine that he involved members of his family because he was in a panic. What to do with the body and how to dispose of it? I guess that's why he sought help from family members."

Even the judge expressed his lack of insight into this question. When speaking of Jonathan Legris, he said, "He was prepared to do anything for his father, that is obvious. My view is I still have not heard the full truth of what his father told him."

Jonathan's tears when being questioned and the fact that he told detectives about the dumped Punto suggests some contrition on his behalf. The court was told that Irene Smith was "totally and utterly ashamed" to have found herself in prison, and that Jonathan followed his father out of "misplaced familial loyalty". Nevertheless, it is hard not to wonder how he had talked them round. Did he admit he had killed Rui Li? Did he say it was an accident? Or were they, as the prosecution suggested, all in financial difficulties and tempted by a life insurance payout?

For all his cold deviousness and mastery of bending family members to his will, Legris was nowhere near as clever as he thought he was. Committing and cleaning up a cold-blooded murder came easily to him. And that seems about as far as he had thought it through. Leaving Rui Li's remains in his son's car in a public place for several days exposed the heartless stupidity of Legris's scheme. The moment he walked into Bournemouth police station to report her missing, his plot started to fall apart and he was in trouble. As desk officer Steve Coward pointed out, you did not need to be Sherlock Holmes to deduce that Legris was shifty and lying. "He's done her in," was Coward's reaction. His last word on the encounter: "Legris was a bad man and a very, very poor liar. Ultimately, that's why he got caught."

The *Daily Echo*, one of Bournemouth's local newspapers, published a report of the Legris trial. In the online comments section, residents who had encountered Legris and his garage were scathing. Legris is called "very sleazy" by one woman who claimed to know him, while others described the garage service as a rip-off, one reader even saying a woman used to stand outside it with a placard warning motorists to stay clear of the service. One man said he had been employed there by Legris and had left within days because of his fiery temper. Another reader said she had met Rui Li, a demurely dressed and dignified woman, who had registered at a language school, possibly – the reader speculated – to improve her life and escape her "bullying, bigamous husband. So sad to see her reputation dragged through the mud in this trial."

As is always the case with such domestic murders, a selfish, emotionless killing wrecked the lives of others and caused untold grief.

Many expressed sadness and sympathy for Rui Li. Her colleagues at Poole Hospital said, "Rui was very conscientious, reliable and had a great attitude to her work. She was well respected by colleagues and patients alike, and is hugely missed as a valuable part of the family on the ward."

Her daughter, Lu Yao, said, "My mum was a wonderful person, a great teacher and the perfect mother to me. I will always love and respect her unconditionally. She will always be in my heart and she is missed every day.

"She worked hard all her life to provide for me, ensuring that I had the best possible upbringing."

MATHEW HARDMAN

Anglesey

6

"He could go round in his home town killing people because he was a vampire"

Anglesey, 2001
Victim: Mabel Leyshon
Murderer: Mathew Hardman

Sometimes a murder occurs that is so far on the extreme limits of normal human behaviour that it disturbs the most experienced detectives and psychiatric experts. The island of Anglesey, off the north Wales coast, had the misfortune to be the setting for such an unsettling murder in 2001.

Reached via two bridges, the Britannia Bridge and the Menai Suspension Bridge, Anglesey is a haven for lovers of the outdoors, pensioners and holidaymakers. It features a number of historic landmarks, including the 13th century Beaumaris Castle, a World Heritage Site, and the spectacular South Stack Lighthouse. Anglesey Island covers 260 square miles and is the second most populous UK island after the Isle of Man, with a population of around 70,000. Most locals are habitual Welsh speakers. Devotees of water sports, hiking, golf and cycling are among those drawn there.

On a quiet Sunday, 25 November, in the mid-afternoon, a crime was uncovered that dismayed and terrified the islanders. Detective Superintendent Alan Jones was called to the home of a pensioner. The 90-year-old lived in a village famed for having the longest place name in Europe – Llanfairpwllgwyngyllgoge rychwyrndrobwllllantysiliogogogoch – known for convenience as Llanfair PG. Jones was not on call that day, but recognised that this was an incident that required urgent attention.

"The events as told to me were that there was an elderly lady, now known to be Mabel Leyshon, aged 90, living at a property by herself," Jones said. "She'd been visited by Meals on Wheels at Sunday lunchtime to take her hot food. Not getting an answer at the front door, the lady delivering the food had gone to the back and seen broken glass and a broken window, became quite rightly concerned, called the police, and there was an emergency response by the local uniformed police. They entered the premises and then as a result of what they saw, it was called in and a major crime investigation was commenced."

The uniformed officers who entered the bungalow on a road called Lon Pant would probably never have experienced such an appalling scene. Even senior investigator Jones was taken aback: "It was quite a difficult scene to interpret at first. Very, very bloodstained. An elderly lady in a chair – turned out that she'd been

MABEL LEYSHON

stabbed 22 times. There was a lot of blood." A couple of candlesticks had been put on the floor, pokers taken from the fireplace and placed in the shape of a cross in front of Mabel Leyshon's chair. "There were a couple of other items that were of concern to us," Jones said, "a saucepan, some newspaper in the saucepan. All of this was examined, and it took quite some time before the full version of events unfolded.

"It was absolutely savage and brutal, and something that was a shock to all of us."

Home Office pathologist Dr Brian Rodgers was called in by North Wales Police. He recalled his journey to Anglesey: "A chilling mist had descended over the Menai Bridge. I felt like I was driving into a real-life horror movie – and I was."

Dr Rodgers was briefed and shown a video taken at the bungalow in preparation for visiting the crime scene. Wearing a protective suit to avoid contaminating evidence, he joined investigators to assess what had happened.

The pathologist described the scene he found. "Mabel Leyshon lived in a very smart bungalow. An elderly lady, and I think, if I remember, her husband, who had died, was a retired veterinary surgeon. So she was obviously quite a well-to-do lady. And it was a quiet area. It's not what you expect to happen in Llanfair PG."

Mabel had been sitting on a sofa armchair – her glasses were on the armrest and various magazines were open there, including a *TV Times* or *Radio Times*. She had been laid out on another armchair facing the doorway as visitors walked in. The pathologist said, "And it immediately became obvious that this was a rather odd scene, to say the least. One thing that took your eye right in front of the fireplace was a candlestick and two cross pokers. And then to the side of that, in the armchair, the body of the victim was slumped in the chair on her back, with the feet resting on a small pouffe."

The full horror of the murder then became apparent. "It was clear that attempts had been made to open up her body in a number of areas, with the idea of possibly draining blood from her," Dr Rodgers said. "A number of the larger wounds were post-mortem [after death]. And then there were a number of stab wounds and defensive wounds. By that, I mean wounds to the arms and the hands, which you will see when a victim tries to ward off an attacker – they put their hands up, they will get injuries to the forearms, the hands, particularly if they try and grab a knife blade coming at them.

"So, as well as those, it was also obvious that there was a huge wound to the chest. You couldn't see it very well, but it was clear that the breastbone, the sternum, had been split open and the cavity beneath, where you would normally expect to see the heart, looked empty. It became clear that the heart was not in her body, and to the right of her feet was a silver platter full of fresh blood and blood clot, with a pan sitting in that and a newspaper-wrapped object. The suspicion was that could be her heart. We unwrapped all the newspaper, and that was the heart. It had been fairly roughly removed."

Wounds were also found to the neck and backs of the legs, part of the killer's perverse attempt to drain blood.

It seemed extraordinary that a little 90-year-old woman, just four feet eleven inches tall, could put up a considerable fight to defend herself in such terrifying circumstances, but Mabel Leyshon had done so.

The splatter around the saucepan suggested that blood had been dripped into it.

Dr Rodgers decided to examine everything forensically at the mortuary, performing an examination of the wrapping and photographing the heart as it was unwrapped. All items were packaged in evidence bags and taken to the mortuary along with the body. For the pathologist, this was an unprecedented scene. He had seen worse, but none where the body had been mutilated after death for an as yet unknown purpose.

The body was taken to a mortuary on the mainland in Bangor. The pathologist did his examination in the early hours of the morning. Here, one of the most bizarre and disturbing aspects of the crime was revealed. "A large number of forensic exhibits and samples would be taken by me," Dr Rodgers said. "We're trying to get DNA trace evidence from the body. And then with the crime-scene investigators, I would photograph all the injuries, and document and track them. I think there were 22 stab wounds, and that's not including all these injuries whereby there'd been attempts to open up various parts of her body, which seemed unusual unless whoever was carrying that out was trying to drain her of her blood. And that was my impression. The distribution of these wounds after death were, in my view, clearly an attempt to drain blood from her body."

Which raised the question: was the perpetrator someone with medical expertise, or a complete amateur? Police would consider the possibility that the killer was a butcher, a veterinary surgeon, even a mortuary technician. "It's really down to whether you need medical knowledge to remove someone's heart," Dr Rodgers said, "and I suppose you could say you needed a certain amount. But is that not available on the internet? That was the difficulty."

Most murder victims have a personal relationship with their killer. This is particularly the case for women. The Office of National Statistics shows that between 2007–08 and 2015–16, more than 70 per cent of female victims knew their attacker. So, who could want to inflict such violence on a quiet retiree such as Mabel? Detectives considered the occult aspects of the crime – the staging of the candlesticks and cross-shaped pokers – as one aspect that could indicate a possible perpetrator.

Alan Jones, who had taken charge of the case as Senior Investigating Officer (SIO), revealed the difficulties he faced: "It was hard to determine at first why anybody would want to stab somebody so brutally. It wasn't clear at the start that anything had been stolen. There was difficulty because she didn't really have any close relatives that she was in constant contact with. So, we had to try and determine whether anything was stolen from the premises, and that seemed not to be the case. But

DETECTIVE
SUPERINTENDENT
ALAN JONES

it became clear to me that we were looking for somebody who had some degree of derangement, mental illness, or something perhaps that happened in the past that may have come to the notice of the public or the police."

As Christmas approached, residents of Llanfair PG and Anglesey locked their windows and doors in dread of another horrific attack. Detectives tried to allay their fears and assured people they were pursuing several lines of inquiry.

The murder team consulted two criminal psychologists to generate a profile of the kind of killer they might be seeking. Det Supt Jones said this suggested a "male, probably 30- or 40-ish, but that there would be some degree of derangement – and to consider occult practices, these sorts of things. So, there was a lot for us to look at." There were several meat-processing factories on Anglesey, and police focused their inquiries there for a time, in the belief that whoever was responsible had access to butchery knives and experience of butchery. That didn't turn out to be the case, but these were all lines of inquiry that had to be made and discounted.

One aspect of the crime scene that puzzled investigators was the significance of the saucepan containing the blood. Det Supt Jones wanted it forensically examined, but this presented a dilemma. Ideally, the pan should be checked for fingerprints or DNA, but examining it for both could destroy either piece of evidence. In the event, it was painstakingly examined by the Forensic Science Service and a strange discovery was made. There was a human lip mark on the saucepan. "It became apparent that whoever was responsible had most probably drunk the blood of the deceased," Jones said.

The satanic elements, brutality of the assault and mutilation of a defenceless elderly woman made this one of Britain's most rare and heinous murders. "To say it was one to shock is a bit of an understatement," said Dr Rodgers. "In all honesty, Llanfair PG is a small community and to have an elderly lady not only murdered but then mutilated in this manner was totally bizarre for anywhere, let alone a place on Anglesey."

The mood on the island was one of horror and worry that the offender was still out and about on the island. The police ran local patrols to reassure the public that they were active and trying their best to find the killer. People had burglar alarms fitted, Age Concern asked residents to keep in touch with elderly neighbours, and closed-circuit television was installed in the village.

It was a headline-grabbing investigation, particularly in Wales, where it was splashed on the front page of the *The Daily Post*. Reporter Eryl Crump was told by one police contact, "If I told you what was found in that house you would never believe me."

Another officer said, "The devil has been to Anglesey."

Almost four weeks into a manhunt that had so far failed to turn up a compelling suspect, Det Supt Jones turned to the media. "I've always worked closely with the media to seek their assistance for anything that might have happened in the preceding months or even years in the locality that concerned the public," he said.

Anglesey was a relatively small and close community, and the media was now key to enlisting the help of local residents. Jones also suspected that the murderer was based near to Mabel Leyshon's home. "It's a peaceful place," he said, "not subject to a lot of crime. We made a point of reminding the community that there wasn't much crime committed within the island. A lot of people know each other, but we were looking to the community to help us solve the crime."

He was not necessarily anticipating reports of crime-related activity, but any behaviour that might have struck members of the public as out of the ordinary. BBC *Crimewatch* and the local press were among the outlets he turned to. It was just before Christmas when Det Supt Jones appeared on *Crimewatch*. He told viewers this was the most horrific murder he had dealt with in his 25 years' experience. A further public appeal was made in January, and the strategy worked, as hundreds of people got in touch.

One reported incident from a couple of months before Mabel's murder stood out. A foreign student said a young man had asked her to bite his neck and had talked about vampirism and vampires. Jones said, "We wanted to trace that foreign student. She turned out to be a German student, and she had a lot of useful information to give to us."

This was the breakthrough the investigation badly needed. Jones explained what happened next: "She gave us the name of Mathew Hardman, and told us that he had talked about vampirism and about how, if you were a vampire, Llanfair PG would be an ideal place to be because there were a lot of elderly people and sources of blood.

"Now, we could have taken that with a pinch of salt. But I thought if someone is acting that strangely, then we should consider at least tracing them, interviewing them, and eliminating them from our inquiry. So, we took a full statement from the German student."

Mathew Hardman did not fit the profile of someone who would murder a pensioner in the extreme way Mabel Leyshon had been killed. He was 17 years old, an art student. For a teenager said to be into vampirism, he did not dress in the style of goth subculture – no dark clothes, dark eye makeup or references to Bram Stoker's *Dracula*. Hardman looked perfectly average. He had two older sisters and lived with his mum, Julia, a nurse, and stepfather, Alan Benneyworth, a former Ministry of Defence fireman. They lived in the same village as Mabel Leyshon, residing about a quarter of a mile from her bungalow. Hardman had been born on the north coast of Anglesey, at a place called Amlwch. In 1998, when he was 13, his family moved to Llanfair PG. His father, who was separated from his mother, died that year from an asthma attack. The loss was said to have distressed Hardman, who had been close to his father. He was also dyslexic, which may help to explain why he studied art, a subject that often brings out the visual skills of people with the learning disability.

Clinical forensic psychologist Professor Mike Berry highlights how far Hardman was from being a likely suspect.

"If I was faced with this case of a 90-year-old woman stabbed 22 times, I would not have been looking for a fantasist who is into vampires. I would probably have thought more of robbery or some sexual behaviour. Seventeen-year-olds don't normally kill old people. It's more likely to be someone their own age. It's more likely to be impulsive, a fight, or sexually based, that kind of stuff. To kill somebody because you want their blood is extremely rare. For a 17-year-old, it's unheard of, basically. So, he's unusual, to say the least, and that made it difficult for the police because they didn't know originally that they were looking for somebody who was into vampires and fantasies."

CLINICAL FORENSIC
PSYCHOLOGIST
PROFESSOR MIKE BERRY

Senior investigator Jones said, "We kept him under surveillance for a time to get some of his habits, his movements. We found out that he was studying at the local college and was living at home with his mother. So we decided that we would do a full search of the premises. We would arrest Mathew at his home address in the early hours of the morning. We made sure, first of all, that he was inside the premises. We would do a full crime-scene examination."

During the search, police took away his footwear. Then came the big find – in the youth's bedroom was a knife. Tests would reveal that it had Mabel Leyshon's blood on it. Another breakthrough came when the Forensic Science Service examined the rear of the pensioner's bungalow, where the killer had broken in. The culprit had left blood staining on the windowsill. "More interestingly," Jones said, "within the blood staining was also DNA, and that was Mathew Hardman's DNA." So, traces of Mabel's blood had been found in Hardman's bedroom, while his DNA was discovered at her home. Subsequently, his trainers matched prints at her premises as well.

So, as unlikely as it initially appeared that teenage Hardman could be the ritualistic killer police were hunting, this evidence was damning. What was the detective's first impression of him? "Surprisingly, he didn't seem bothered, didn't seem fazed by it all. In fact, if anything, he seemed to enjoy the whole experience, from arrest through interviews to being charged. He never admitted to the offence, but he was quite content to talk to the interviewing officers."

Investigators were piecing together a more coherent picture of the young killer and his connection to Mabel. She was, Det Supt Jones said, a "very proud lady. Very smart, very tidy, kept herself to herself. The premises were kept in good order. We did find a link between Mathew Hardman and her, in that he had in the past been delivering a free newspaper to her premises, and he had, in fact, spoken to her at the premises." He denied killing her, however.

Jones and his team were nevertheless relieved that they had gone ahead with the arrest of Hardman. In addition to the footprint, knife and DNA evidence, they found signs of his obsession with the occult and vampirism – books, magazines and sites visited on his computer. Prof Berry said, "Without any doubt, when the police eventually consider him a suspect and go to his house, they find material there far in excess of what the ordinary teenager would have. An ordinary teenager would have a few photographs, maybe the odd magazine, but they wouldn't have it to the extent that he did, the intensity of his interest. That's the key thing, this belief that went beyond reality about vampires. This was quite frightening and worrying, because there is very little anybody would have known about it. You would not have predicted that this guy would kill."

Hardman's secret fixation on vampires was one part of his mentality. Criminal psychologist Dr Donna Youngs points to another component in his homicidal worldview. "The existence of the kind of material that we know Mathew Hardman collected and devoured on the occult will have played a role in what he went on to do," she said. "But the reason it was allowed to have this impact upon him was because of a pre-existing psychological dysfunction within him, which was this inability to see other people as fully human. Normally, a healthy person would have other people. In the narrative of Mathew Hardman, I don't think there are any parts written for other people. Other people just don't figure, don't exist in his personal narrative, and I think that's what we've seen here, with the cutting out of the heart and so forth. He sees other people without any humanity whatso-ever. And when he became interested in the occult, that simply channelled this profound psychological dysfunction that already existed into this type of horrific offending."

A chilling factor here is how detached from reality he became. "He asked a 16-year-old girl to bite him on the neck because he was convinced," Prof Berry said, "based on no logic or any sensible ideas, that she was a vampire. She was going to bite him and then make him a vampire. Then he could go round in his home town killing people because he was a vampire."

Tragically, Mabel Leyshon was drawn into his appalling fantasy. Despite having known her for several years, Hardman had no qualms about attacking her. "He knew her, he knew the house, and I imagine he knew he would get in quite easily," Prof Berry said. "So, what he's done was quite cold-blooded, but also lazy. Most killers move a further distance from their home area to start their killing. To kill literally on your doorstep increases the risks of being caught."

Mold Crown Court heard the full story of Mathew Hardman's evolution from teenage student to fantasist and murderer. A boy who had known Hardman at school described him as a "normal lad" to the court. He was not particularly sociable, the witness said: Hardman stayed in at home most of the time. He had had a paper round from the ages of 13 to 16, which included Mabel's bungalow.

Because of his dyslexia, Hardman had had a special needs tutor, who told the jury he had been well behaved, with a good sense of humour. Hardman left David Huws School at the age of 16 to study art and design at Menai College. In addition to college, he had a part-time job as a kitchen porter. A friend said his home featured nothing strange that might indicate he could be a killer. When it came to his art portfolio, however, friends said it was filled with "morbid and depressing" images, revolving around death, blood and knives.

The court also heard about his disconcerting encounter on 23 September 2001, two months before the murder, with the German exchange student, aged 16, whom he was convinced was a vampire. In addition to asking her to bite him, he had said Anglesey was perfect for vampires because there were many pensioners there who could be killed for their blood. People would assume, he suggested, they had died of heart attacks.

It also emerged that Hardman had been arrested for his behaviour during his encounter with the German student. He had visited the girl at her lodgings. When she refused to bite him, he had become violent and had to be dragged away by the landlady of the lodgings, who called the police. This was after Hardman had punched himself on the nose and asked the two women to smell his blood. Sergeant Peter Nicholson said he asked the lad to leave peacefully. "He didn't make any sort of coherent response," the sergeant said. "All he could say was, 'bite my neck'."

Hardman continued to deny he was the murderer, as he did when he was arrested. He had turned to his sobbing mother, as the arresting officers were about to take him away, and said, "It's all right, Mum, I didn't do anything." The prosecution, however, detailed the compelling evidence against Hardman in the form of his DNA on Mabel Leyshon's windowsill, the bloodstained knife in his bedroom, and marks from his Levi's trainers at her bungalow.

At the end of a 14-day hearing, and after four hours of deliberation, the jury were unanimous in finding Hardman guilty of the savage murder. As the verdict was announced, it was Hardman's turn to start crying as his mother wailed in the public gallery. The judge, Mr Justice Richards, ordered that he be detained at Her Majesty's pleasure, a life sentence with a minimum term of 12 years. Mr Justice Richards said, "It was planned and carefully calculated. Why you, an otherwise pleasant and well-regarded young man, should act in this way is difficult to comprehend. You had hoped for immortality. All you achieved was to brutally end another person's life, and the bringing of a life sentence upon yourself."

North Wales Police Chief Constable Richard Brunstrom revealed how challenging the case had been for the 60 officers involved. "It was a particularly difficult investigation because of the awful circumstances. It was an unpleasant case, which the officers had to get very close to – in terms of dealing with the relatives and the appalling scene itself. We are human beings just like anybody else, but have to retain a sense of professional detachment. We cannot collapse in horror and recoil – it was a psychological challenge."

After the trial, Hardman's former girlfriend told a local newspaper that she had been taunted at school after his arrest. "I was his girlfriend for three months – on and off – last year," she is reported to have said. "He was quiet, really kind. I felt gutted when I heard he had been arrested. I don't think he's really up to doing anything like that."

The youngsters had shared a passion for the rock music of Marilyn Manson, a controversial figure whose name is a juxtaposition of the names of film star Marilyn Monroe and

Charles Manson, whose followers committed mass murder. "He did my art homework for me," the ex-girlfriend said. "I've still got that. It was called the Apocalypse."

There is a level of plain unknowability to Mathew Hardman. Forensic psychologists and psychiatrists can inch us closer to some insight into his inexplicable behaviour and brutality, but even after he was locked up, he still continued to perplex.

Chris Kinealy was the admissions nurse at Altcourse Prison in Liverpool, where he dealt with prisoners on referral from 1998 to 2010. He was stunned by his first encounter with the youth. He said, "I was told this young boy was coming through and he was accused of a heinous murder." Even for a high-security prison such as Altcourse, the horror of Hardman's crime was unusual. "I was asked to interview him by the admissions manager, who asked me to have a prison officer with me. I didn't want that, but he insisted.

PSYCHIATRIC NURSE
CHRIS KINEALY

"Mathew Hardman walked into the little room, which I had as my office, stood there with a very pleasant grin on his face. Young, handsome, long blond hair, blue eyes, bit of acne. Very well spoken. Asked me if I was the doctor. I explained I was the psychiatric nurse. He sat down. Very pleasant, easy to talk to, and I said, how do you feel? And he said, "This is the most exciting thing that's ever happened to me." I was absolutely flabbergasted when he said that, but you learn to keep a straight face. We chatted for about an hour. He seemed totally unconcerned about the situation he was in. He treated it all as a huge joke."

This was while Hardman was still 17 and on remand. He was placed on the hospital wing because the prison was intended for those who had turned 18.

Kinealy recalled, "He spent nearly a year on the hospital wing. I spoke to him sometimes three times a week. He never admitted responsibility for the crime, and he maintained this air of absolute total indifference.

"Whenever I spoke to him, he would say it's a mistake. The judge did comment that he was convicted on overwhelming evidence. That was the expression the judge used. I walked into his cell and he was curled up in a foetal position, crying, and I said, 'You'll be getting shipped from here, Mathew. The only advice I can give you is keep your head down and behave yourself, because you're an infamous criminal, you're going to be well known in the YP – young prison – the institution that you go to.' And he asked me, 'Do you think I'm guilty?' And I said, 'Yes, I do. Everybody thinks you're guilty. I know you're guilty.' And he just burst into tears and curled up in tears again. That was the only time I ever saw him display any emotion."

For Kinealy, Hardman's demeanour was exceptional, and it stuck with him. People entering prison for the first time, particularly younger offenders, display several types of behaviour. For some it is defiance: I don't care, give me life, so what? Others might be in tears – I want my mum, my solicitor, a doctor. Putting on a show of bravado might be easy if you are in for shoplifting or smashing windows.

"But he knew what he was accused of: the most heinous crime imaginable," Kinealy said. "When I was 17, I was a big strapping lad, but if I'd been taken to prison, charged with murder, I would have been in floods of tears. He just seemed to think it was all a huge joke."

Hardman's indifference to being in prison also struck Prof Berry. The clinical forensic psychologist said, "When he was taken into prison he enjoyed the whole process. It was the best experience he'd had in his life. Now, that is very strange, because you've got a 17-year-old boy who had been weeping at his trial when he got a life sentence. And yet within days he's saying how much he enjoys prison. Does prison give him the safety and security he didn't feel at home? We know he had a mother and stepfather, he had a nice stable home – and yet he's looking for something else."

In all the conversations the young prisoner had with his psychiatric nurse, he never discussed his motive for his monstrous crime. He never talked about vampirism or satanism. But Chris Kinealy found the contradictions in him hard to reconcile. Hardman was intelligent, but had left many clues at the crime scene as to his identity. It was almost as if he was coasting on a wave of delusion and unreality, expecting to breeze out of court having been deemed innocent. Then, once in prison, he seemed oblivious to the revulsion he had caused with his crime.

"Of all the interviews I've done, and I've interviewed tens of thousands of inmates coming into prisons, he sticks in my mind," Kinealy said. "I remember him vividly. He was extremely convincing and extremely dangerous. When a boy commits a serious crime, you obviously look for motives. There was no motive whatsoever in this crime, except for the occult. It wasn't sexual, it wasn't gang related, it wasn't drugs. It was a young boy who all on his own committed the most horrible crime imaginable on a totally innocent old lady. You ask yourself why? And the only reason is an insane one, that he thought he'd be a vampire and live forever. And I'm convinced he thought when it went to court he would just get not guilty and he'd walk out laughing. He didn't, and that's why that particular day he was showing emotion. This was his first real contact with reality when the judge gave him life imprisonment. When he got that [sentence], it came home to him. But his lack of emotion in itself was a symptom of a mental illness, I'm sure."

Kinealy referred Hardman to a psychiatrist as a matter of urgency. He was seen by one, but he still ended up in the normal prison system, suggesting that if he had mental health problems they have probably not been treated. "I would have said someone like that needed transfer to a high-security mental hospital," Kinealy said. He subsequently heard from another inmate that after being transferred to Moorland prison and young offender institution, Hardman – categorised as a vulnerable prisoner – was attacked on a couple of occasions by other prisoners. He had since gone to the gym and fought back against assailants. After that he was generally left alone.

In 2017 there were media reports that Hardman was among a number of notorious murderers who had been told that they would never be released. This followed a European Court of Human Rights judgment that whole-life terms were not in violation of Article 3 of the European Convention of Human Rights. It will be a matter of rejoicing for most people that he will be shut away for good, but his ghastly crime leaves one question hanging that will likely never be resolved. How was it that a young man from an apparently stable background, with no evidence of having been abused, could turn himself into the perpetrator of such a distressing crime?

Det Supt Alan Jones had the satisfaction of catching Hardman, a killer he was sure would have committed further murders had he not been arrested, but he remained bewildered by the youth he took into custody. "Still difficult to believe how anybody could be influenced in that way to carry out such a macabre, such a savage beating of a vulnerable, elderly lady within his own community," he said. "He only lived a short distance from her, so I do find it difficult to understand why."

For Chris Kinealy, the young killer will always be one of the most extraordinary encounters of his time as a psychiatric nurse. He said, "The thing that sticks in my mind is when he walked through the door and stood and smiled at me. He was a young, handsome, well-spoken lad. And if – I haven't got any daughters – but if my daughter had brought him home and said, 'Dad, this is Mathew, I've just met him,' I would have thought, *Oh, well, what a nice lad*. And that was someone who had disembowelled an old lady and drunk her blood."

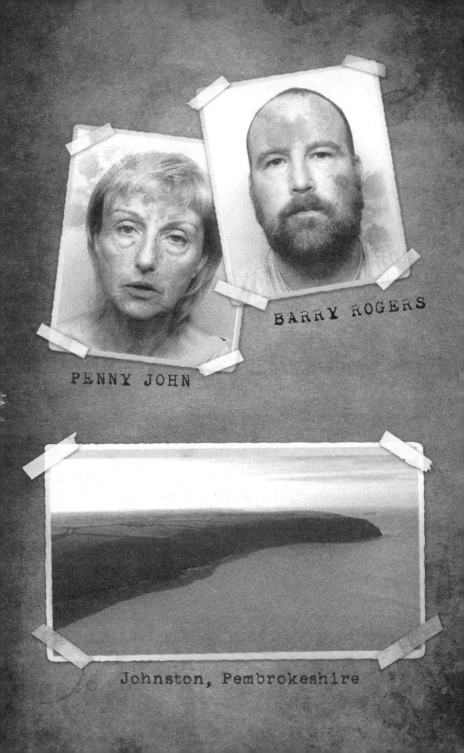

PENNY JOHN

BARRY ROGERS

Johnston, Pembrokeshire

7

"I definitely feel like I had a lucky escape"

Johnston, Pembrokeshire, 2011
Victim: Betty Guy
Murderers: Penelope John and Barry Rogers

Rhianne Morris came into contact with Barry Rogers in the summer of 2010 via the dating site Zoosk. She had just turned 19 and had recently become a mother. Her daughter was three months old. Rhianne and Barry messaged each other for a couple of weeks.

"Online, he was the best thing since sliced bread," she recalled. "He made me feel beautiful. I felt frumpy, I felt ugly. I felt, you know, I've got a baby from somebody, no one will want me now. And he made me feel like a princess."

She had been spending a lot of time in her flat with her baby. She had not been going out to meet anyone and hoped that the dating site might help her to find a new partner. Eventually, she and Barry met up in Bath for the first time.

"Barry had a presence," she said. "We met in a train station, where there were hundreds of people, and I knew it was him as soon as he walked towards me. He seemed polite, kind, very interested."

Like most young mums, Rhianne was still finding her way with parenthood. "I didn't have a clue what I was doing when it came to bathing, burping and all that kind of thing, and he came and swept me off my feet and showed me how easy it was."

A couple of weeks after meeting Barry, Rhianne travelled to Cardigan on the north Pembrokeshire coast and met Barry's mother, Penelope, who was living in a women's refuge. Penelope had lived in Turkey with Barry's father, who was abusive towards her. Barry told Rhianne that his father would hit Penelope and the family lived in fear of him. "Barry spoke about his childhood when we first met," Rhianne said. "Barry explained that his father was violent to Penelope, and that everybody was on eggshells. Barry and his younger brother would have to watch what they said and did because, if not, Penelope would be the one that would be in trouble for that."

Barry Rogers had been the eldest of three children. Penelope John had had him when she was 17 years old. Barry had gone to school in west Wales, before leaving at 17 to join the army. He spent a couple of years with the Royal Corps of Signals, doing one tour of Iraq in 2005.

Of Penelope, Rhianne said, "My first impression – really jittery, friendly, couldn't do enough for you. She was very familiar, very quickly."

Penelope's relationship with Barry was unlike any mother-son bond Rhianne had ever seen. "Super, super friendly, cuddly, kissy," she said. "They'd hold hands. She sat on his lap. He'd smack her bum. It was quite an experience.

Barry and Penny were almost too close for a mother and son relationship. At the start, I just gathered that that was normal for them."

She also witnessed Barry with his former girlfriend, with whom he had a child. "I didn't know if any of Barry's previous relationships were troubled or violent or anything. I only knew about him and the mother of his child, and they still shared a good enough relationship to co-parent for the sake of his child."

He told Rhianne about his experiences in the army, during which he mentioned post-traumatic stress disorder and that Iraq had affected his mental health. Rhianne could sympathise with that: "I'm an ex-army child myself. My father served twice, so I had sympathy for him that he'd had to experience that at a young age, and that kind of explained why he was so snappy and how things affected him."

Rhianne also learned more about Penelope's background. The details she picked up were that Penelope had a pleasant upbringing with her mother and father, and then the parents separated. She also heard how awful Penelope's life was with Barry's father, her "first love", who she met when she was 16. Apparently, her time in Turkey got so bad that officials stepped in to help them leave the country, even though they did not have passports.

"I felt like I had a responsibility then to be the calm, loving person that they both needed," Rhianne said. She wanted to be the level-headed voice if there were heated moments or arguments. Rhianne soon found, however, that this was a lot to shoulder. "As a young single mum, having to bring up my child and then look out for Barry and then Penny, to see that we were all getting along fine in a healthy relationship, was a lot of pressure at that age."

When it came to who had final say in decision-making between mother and son, it was generally Barry who got his way. But Rhianne continued to be bemused by how odd their affinity was. "Barry and Penny's relationship day-to-day was weird, un-boundaried, they were constantly looking for an OK from each other as to the way to behave with each other and with life. They definitely had a strange relationship."

And then her own relationship with Barry took a nasty turn. No sooner had Rhianne moved into his flat than there were displays of temper, and it was Rhianne who was treading on eggshells. Three months into their life as a couple, he hit her for the first time.

"I felt so isolated," she said of this dismal period. "All I had was my daughter, Barry and Penny. If I wanted to talk to anyone, it would be Penny. If I needed to make a friend, I'd have to ask him – I've met this person, I think they would be a good friend, and he'd shoot them down. No, they're a horrible person. So, it was just me. Whatever Barry said I could do, whoever I could talk to, that was what I had to do."

She spoke of her unhappiness to Penelope. Barry made her feel cut off, stuck in the flat. He hit her. Penelope's response was that it was best not to wind him up. If she needed to confide in anyone, she should speak to Penelope. Rhianne initially felt Penelope was her ally. After all, she had been in a violent relationship herself and come through it. She might know best how to deal with Barry.

However, Penelope's advice was no help at all. "The abuse I received from Barry lasted the entire relationship. It was more mental abuse than physical. And that's why I didn't really realise that that's what was happening. It wasn't until I was out that I realised it was all wrong."

Rhianne did find some relief when she visited Penelope's mother, 84-year-old Betty Guy. She recalled, "Betty was a beautiful, beautiful person. She reminded me of Miss Honey from *Matilda* [the Roald Dahl story], that if she did grow old, that's exactly who Betty was. She was just a little old lady who did nothing but love and care and make everybody feel welcome. When I spent time in Betty's house, I knew that it was calm, that I could say what I liked, that nothing was going to happen to me. I just felt comfort. That was one place where I felt comfortable."

Betty lived in Johnston, three miles inland from the coast at Milford Haven in Pembrokeshire. She told Rhianne she had been a nurse in the army. Even in her eighties, she

volunteered at a charity shop. "Her entire life, in my eyes, revolved around everybody but herself," Rhianne said. "I don't know one single person that wouldn't describe Betty as a lovely, caring human being." When she visited the grandmother along with Barry and Penelope, Betty was the matriarchal

RHIANNE MORRIS, PRIME
WITNESS IN THE BETTY
GUY MURDER TRIAL

figure, the one who they were all there to see and who was a shrewd judge of character. Rhianne never told her about being hit or controlled by Barry, but she felt that Betty sensed what was going on. Gran made her feel welcome and secure in her home.

Penelope was close to her mother, and Betty loved Barry too, in Rhianne's estimation, though she probably did not condone everything he did.

One issue Betty had was her health. She talked about her poor health often and the fact that she was struggling. She could be "down in the dumps" about her well-being, Rhianne said. "Barry possibly thought Betty was a burden. She, you know, took time from his life that he could have spent elsewhere. However, I felt Penelope loved to go and tend to her. That's what kept her busy." While there were occasions when the mood was, *Uh, we've got to go down to see nan*, Rhianne knew of no arguments between the granny and Penelope and Barry.

When it came to the mother-son touchy-feely rapport, Betty, however, did not approve. "There were definitely behaviours in front of Betty that she didn't agree with," Rhianne said. "Penelope would sit on Barry's lap, he'd cuddle her in, they'd kiss on the lips. There were definite things like that that Betty didn't like in our presence."

One night, shortly before bedtime, in November 2011, when Barry and Rhianne were at home in Frome, Somerset, the phone rang as they were watching the television. Rhianne could see "Mum" – Penelope – on the phone's display, which was on the sofa between them. Rhianne said, "He answered the phone, she said something, and then he said, 'Oh, it's time, is it?' and walked out the room. When he reappeared, he had a bag packed and he was quite irrationally running around, putting stuff in a bag, and said, 'My nan's really ill, I'm going to have to go.'"

Later that night she heard from Barry again. He called to say his nan had died. "I felt sad for Betty and gutted for Barry," Rhianne said. "Barry's emotional state on the phone was that he was upset. He obviously was drunk or something because he was slurring his words. But I didn't know at the time that he was drunk until after. I thought he was just very upset. He was over-talking, like blabbering. I was just like, 'Oh, it's OK, you know, these things happen, at least she's not in pain anymore.' And it was like he had to keep going over the same point, where we had the same conversation about three times on the phone."

He gave no explanation about what had happened with Betty, so Rhianne assumed the cancer she had heard Betty was suffering with had finally killed her. When he returned, he said they needed to pack and go to stay at Penelope's in St Dogmaels, near Cardigan. When they arrived, Penelope was with a friend, drinking coffee with whisky in it, reminiscing about her mother. Rhianne noticed some awkward silences when she entered a room, but thought that was down to how upset Penny and Barry were. She did her best to be strong for Barry, his mum and his younger brother, Charlie. She also took on the mundane household tasks during this period, such as tidying the kitchen. At the same time, Rhianne was affected by the loss of Betty herself. "I did definitely feel that I'd lost a member of my family also, because of who Betty was to me and how she kept me going."

Rhianne was not involved in the arrangements for the cremation, all of which seemed to be in place. One point that struck her was how quickly it was carried out, with just four days between Betty's death and the funeral. "I thought it was quite rushed. I remember thinking about my nan passing and there were at least three weeks before we even had a slot for her to be cremated. So, for Betty to have died and been cremated within four days, I thought was rather quick, but I wasn't one to judge or let my opinion be known."

The day of the service also held surprises. Rhianne got the impression the event was thrown together, and she was not aware that some of the family had not been informed the funeral was taking place. "I thought everybody knew. And it wasn't until we got to the crematorium that I knew that Penny noticed her sister was there and wasn't very happy about that. I felt quite awkward to be at somebody's funeral where there was clearly animosity in the air."

And there had been another surprise before the funeral. Betty was laid out in an open casket at a chapel of rest in the days before the funeral. Barry, Penny, Charlie and Rhianne, along with her daughter, went in to pay their respects. Rhianne kissed Betty goodbye on the forehead. She was struck by how beautiful the grandmother looked. She was dressed impeccably, hair done beautifully, with full makeup. It turned out that

Penny had dressed and done her makeup. "I found it weird that anyone would want to be that close to their deceased mother, to the point that you wash them and dress them and put their makeup on and do their hair. However, Penny was very overfamiliar, so it wasn't completely out of character for her to do something like that. But I definitely found it strange."

The time after the funeral was a particularly dark period for Rhianne. Barry was more pent up than ever, lashing out over anything that irritated him. The beatings got worse. Her relationship with him was the most difficult time she had faced in her life.

With her voice breaking at times, she recalled, "After the funeral, the way Barry behaved with me was so unpredictable. Before, I'd usually be able to walk in and gauge what kind of mood he was in, so then I could amend the way I was talking to him, the way I behaved around him, to not give him any reason to do anything to me. But after the funeral, I just felt like there was no rhyme or reason. It was just if he was in a mood and he felt like he needed to let it out, he let it out.

"I was living in the town where my family live, all of my friends live. Everybody knew me, nobody knew him. And I still felt like I was just trapped on my own."

Penny had just lost her mother, so Rhianne did not feel able to tell her about her son's aggression. So, she kept her feelings to herself.

Unexpectedly, something then happened to allow her to break free of the nightmare. Barry tried to kill himself.

Rhianne called an ambulance, believing he was dead. He survived but was sectioned. Under the Mental Health Act 1983, this usually entails being kept in hospital for a patient's safety until they get treatment.

After nearly two years with Barry, Rhianne was out of the relationship. However, she felt lost. "I was trying to move on with my life. I quickly realised that the way I was thinking wasn't necessarily normal or OK. So I went to the doctor. They referred me for counselling, and then, in turn, for cognitive behavioural therapy, to try and change the way I thought things should be.

"The Barry I met at the beginning was lovely, beautiful, picked me up, showed me how to be a mother, made me feel lovely. Everything you'd want from a man. And the Barry I left at the end was your worst nightmare."

Rhianne carried on the process of making a new life. Eventually, she had another relationship, then another child. She felt as though things were going well and that she had left Barry behind.

Then, around four years after Betty's death, the police arrived at Rhianne's home. "I answered the door. They were plain-clothed, they had laptop bags and ID badges. And I instantly thought, *Oh, I've not paid a bill or these are bailiffs.* And then when they showed me their badges and I saw CID, I guessed it wasn't bailiffs, but I had no idea why they'd be knocking at my door."

Their first question was whether Rhianne had been Barry's partner. She said yes. "And then they said, 'What do you know about the death of Betty Guy?' And I just said, 'That was Barry's nan, and she died from cancer.'"

This reopened some dark feelings for Rhianne. "To hear his name again hit me to the pit of my stomach. I felt sick."

She was also wondering why the detectives would be interested in Betty Guy. "When I told them that I thought she'd died of cancer, they just had blank looks on their faces and asked another question. They didn't say she had or she hadn't. It was kind of like they just needed more information."

Rhianne gave them an account of her entire relationship with Barry, including what she knew of Betty's ill health and her death. "Once I'd given my entire statement, they said to me that they had reason to believe that this wasn't an innocent death, that she'd just died of cancer. They said that they thought she'd been murdered."

Shock on top of shock. Rhianne stumbled over her words at recalling this. "I can't... the words, I don't even think there were words, I was just feeling sick. And then my mind went into overdrive and I thought, *Well, hang on, the way he was with me is not two moons apart from him potentially being able to do something like that.* I didn't know what he was capable of, but I felt sick to think that he would be capable of murdering his own nan."

Her thoughts turned to Betty, whom she remembered as not having a bad bone in her body. It was incomprehensible to Rhianne that Barry or anyone could want to murder her. Even years after these events, she still had heard no reason to explain this.

After the CID officers left, her mind went back to the evening in November 2011 and Barry's "Oh, it's time, is it?"

conversation with Penny, before he left in a hurry. Rhianne's mind was racing with questions. What was that phone call about? "Was that a sign? I can't even... there were just so many things I thought... Could I have stopped it? Like, could I have made this not happen? Or like, is there something I did that... I just can't even tell you what was going through my head."

Further meetings with the police followed. She gave additional statements, added detail to her account.

Then Barry Rogers and Penelope John were charged with the murder of Betty Guy. Rhianne would soon be confronted by the ordeal of facing Barry in court.

Barry, who was living in Fishguard, and Penelope, still residing in St Dogmaels, were arrested, questioned and charged with murder on 18 July 2017. The following January, they went on trial at Swansea Crown Court. They denied the charge.

Prosecutors outlined the facts of their case against the couple: how, in the early hours of 7 November 2011, Barry, aged 22, and Penelope, 50, gave Betty a cocktail of whisky and crushed tablets to make her drowsy. Barry probably then smothered her with a pillow.

Penelope had called the emergency services and said she thought her mother had died. She added that her mother had stomach and bowel cancer. The prosecution said that, on the contrary, Betty's medical history showed she did not have cancer and was not terminally ill. Her GP reported bruising to her legs and mouth, but no post-mortem was carried out. The death certificate stated that Betty died of broncho-pneumonia, septicaemia and hypertensive heart disease.

Considering the case after the trial, clinical forensic psychologist Professor Mike Berry was struck by how out of the ordinary this type of murder was. He said, "Matricide is unusual, to say the least. But to incorporate your son into killing your mother is extremely rare. We don't normally have male and female killing teams, that's very unusual."

With no one suspecting otherwise at this point, the mother and son got away with murder for six years. As the trial continued, the jury would learn a lot more about Betty Guy, Penelope and Barry, and how they were caught.

First, it became clear that, like many 84-year-olds, Betty had several medical issues. These may have lowered her mood occasionally, but she was certainly not at death's door. She had complained to her GP several times of diarrhoea. Eventually, a colorectal surgeon was consulted, and she had two endoscopies. These found that her stomach was normal – she had some bowel inflammation, but there was no cancer.

On 6 November, Betty spoke to her neighbour, Mary Collier, and said she had "had enough". Mrs Collier summoned Penelope. Betty died that night.

Rhianne was one of the prosecution's vital witnesses. However, giving her testimony proved to be a major challenge. The first hurdle was simply summoning the fortitude to agree to appear in court, and for this she was thankful for the assistance she got from the police. "The investigating officers that dealt with me, they were two ladies, fantastic investigators.

In actual fact, if it wasn't for one of them, I would never have given evidence in court. I didn't feel strong enough. I didn't feel like what I had to say would help in any way. So, it was her perseverance, giving me the confidence to let my voice be heard and knowing that nothing would happen to me."

Testifying, however, was still daunting. Rhianne recalled, "The first day of court, the drive up, I couldn't eat, I couldn't drink. I felt so sick. I got there. I've never been to court. I just guessed it was like how they showed it on TV. They kept me calm, they said it's nothing like you see on TV. However, when I walked into that courtroom it was like slow motion. I just felt lost, like, *Why am I here?* And to see all those people, the jury, and then to sit down and see him was sickening.

"Barry stared at me from the moment I walked in the courtroom, all the way around the tables, and as I sat down. I could still see and feel him staring at me the entire time."

She told the court that Barry had had a close relationship with his gran, attempting to cheer her up when she was ill. She also recounted an incident at Betty's home when he had said to Betty, "Don't worry, nan, if it gets too much, I'll finish you off." Rhianne said she took this as a joke and that Betty liked to banter. She added that Penelope had cared for her mother.

Her time on the stand was made all the more difficult because Barry shuffled in his seat so that he could peer over the prosecuting QC's shoulder to stare at her the entire time she was giving evidence.

"The prosecuting QC realised that Barry was intimidating me. He understood that he was looking over his shoulder. So, he reiterated to me that I look at him for the question, and I turn and face the jury to give my answer, which is difficult because there's so many people that you don't know which one to look at. So, I just looked at all of them. And to start with, I felt like the way that the questions were being asked from the defence, the jury thought that they [Penelope and Barry] were innocent and I was evil."

Rhianne told the court about the night when Barry had been called by his mother – "Oh, it's time, is it?" – and had left in a rush. She told how later he had been drinking whisky and was upset. When he was back in Somerset, she asked why, and he replied that his mother had given Betty whisky and tablets, adding, "It made her sleepy."

When describing the period after the funeral and Barry's violent moods, Rhianne said that during one row he told her, "I'll do it in your sleep, no one will know about it," as he held a pillow to his face. "I'll do it to you like I did to her." She did not understand what he was referring to. She was too scared to ask him what he meant.

Johanna Carr, a journalist who covered the trial, recalled one interesting moment from Rhianne's testimony: "Rhianne Morris attended the funeral as Barry Rogers' girlfriend at the time. She was asked by the prosecution whether or not she'd seen any marks on Betty Guy's face. Now this was something the doctor who had examined Betty said he had seen, small pinpoint bruising. Rhianne said no, she couldn't see any marks on Betty's face because her makeup had been done. Now, who had done the makeup? That was Penelope John."

Having been under the impression she would be questioned for 10 minutes, Rhianne found herself on the stand for two and a half hours. The most emotionally devastating moment for her came when Barry and Penny's defence lawyers attempted to destroy her credibility as a witness. The aspect of her relationship they chose to pick on was that Rhianne had got pregnant with Barry's child but decided she had to have an abortion.

"I was 16 weeks four days, but Barry was still hitting me while I was pregnant with his child," she said. "So I did leave and go to Somerset and have an abortion because I felt that that was necessary for myself, my child and my unborn child, that nobody should be part of that. And his defence turned that into: I convinced Barry to fall in love with me, I fell pregnant with his child and then to hurt him, I took myself to Somerset and murdered his child to get at him."

The prosecution attempted to show the other side of this by asking Rhianne about messages Barry had sent her on Facebook. "He used to call me a baby murderer after the abortion while we were still together. And then when we'd split, he got married, and on the day he got married, he sent me a picture of him and his wife via a Facebook message with the caption, 'Well, at least this one isn't a baby murderer.' That hurt, that hurt. The fact he tried to use that as part of his defence, that broke me, hurt deeper than anything."

To compound her distress, she was being hounded by the press, who would be at her front door asking to speak to her.

Rhianne had to change her hairstyle, wear glasses and even duck into her neighbour's house to avoid them at this time.

Despite all this, she came to realise that it was vital to tell what she knew. She was alone in having been with Barry before, during and after his visit to Betty's on the night of the murder. Rhianne felt, in particular, that she needed to testify for Betty. "For justice, for Betty," she said. "If I didn't turn up that day and they got away with it, then I'd just feel so gutted for Betty that she didn't get the justice she deserved."

Sandra Adams, who became Barry's girlfriend after Rhianne, gave evidence next. It was Sandra – who had also been assaulted by Barry during their 10-month relationship – who reported him and Penelope to the police. The reason? Barry had told her he killed somebody. She told the court, "I asked him, was it in the army? And he said, 'No, it wasn't.'

"He then told me that it was his nan that he killed." She told the court he said to her he had driven from Frome in Somerset after receiving a call from his mother telling him "it was time". He had said Betty was terminally ill with cancer and "it was her time to go".

She continued, "He said he went in to his nan and they gave her medication… he waited a little while for the medication to kick in and then he placed a pillow over her face and smothered her. The grandmother was fighting back and he stopped… he had a glass of whisky and then went back to her and placed the pillow back over her face a second time, and she passed away then." So, Barry had made two attempts to smother his 84-year-old granny.

Sandra Adams's mother, Linda Pritchard-Jones, said Barry had confessed the same to her. "He told me that his nan had cancer and that when the time came, his nan had asked him to help her finish her life," she told the court.

Further confirmation of this came from Sandra Adams's sister, Tracey. At a children's birthday party he told her he had "helped his nan along with a pillow".

More damning evidence came from Lisa Watkins, who married Barry in 2014. She told the court, "He asked me my thoughts on euthanasia… and he said his nan had asked him to help her pass." He did not explain how he had done this, but in previous conversations he had also mentioned killing his grandmother. She agreed that he was in the habit of seeking attention and sympathy.

When Rhianne – who had once been incredulous that anyone could want to kill Betty – heard this testimony from Barry's former partners and their relatives, she was stunned. "It sickened me," she said, "to know that I lived next to that man after he'd been capable of something like that."

Next, the court was told that the police had taken the rare step of making covert recordings of Barry and Penelope at her St Dogmaels house. When the police confronted Barry with these during questioning, he claimed unconvincingly to have known they were being recorded and made up his comments to "take the piss out of you pigs". Excerpts were played to the jury. Barry was heard saying, "We deny it, they can't prove anything because there's no evidence, it's all hearsay. It's me that's done the act… you got nothing to worry about, mam."

Penelope is heard fretting over whether there are texts of what she communicated to Barry, no doubt fearing they could be used in evidence against them: "No... I can't remember, did I text you when I said I crushed the diazepam up and crushed the zopiclone up [both drugs are sedatives] and I put it in her... [indecipherable]... No, I wouldn't have texted that to you, Barry... on reflection, I wouldn't have texted you that, I would have told you on the phone."

On Tuesday, 6 February 2018, Penelope and Barry were found guilty of murdering Betty. They were sentenced to life, to serve a minimum of 11 years. Rhianne remembered the trial's climax: "They [Penelope and Barry] broke down in tears, put their heads in their hands – purely out of selfishness that they'd lost their life, not that somebody else had lost their life.

"In my opinion, the sentence was nowhere near long enough for the crime they committed. It wasn't just a random person. This was their family, their nan, their mother. If you're capable of cold-heartedly murdering your own mother or your own nan, anybody else is easy, surely."

When it came to the perplexing question of why they had done it, Mr Justice Lewis said they had a "misguided belief" that "murder was an act of mercy". He said, "This was not a case where Mrs Guy was suffering, or you believed she was suffering in unbearable pain and you wanted to bring that pain to an end... you believed Mrs Guy was old and ill and wanted to die and you believed that you should end her life."

Money had certainly not been the motive. Betty lived in a council flat. A friend, Betty Wilson, said she helped Mrs Guy to claim pension credit, income support and housing benefit. All Betty Guy's daughter inherited was a washing machine and tumble dryer.

The defence said it must have been a "mercy killing", one based on "care and love". Alternatively, it is hard not to conclude it was a stupid and heartless killing. As Betty's friends and relatives made clear after the trial, the grandmother was loved and cherished by many, and her murder had devastated those who had known her. Instead of love and support from her daughter and grandson, Betty had received a distressing, grubby end from the pair.

While Rhianne did not know whose idea the murder might have been originally, she suspected that once it was decided upon, Barry would have been in charge. "Barry took charge of everything," she said.

Lorraine Matthews, Betty's other daughter, had a victim impact statement read out in court. She said her mother had "loved life" and "loved a little giggle". The statement continued, "We grieved once after her death and now we have to go through a different kind of grief." She said she was "shocked that a member of my own family is capable of committing such a despicable act on an old lady".

Finally: "My mother was in no way ill enough to warrant a mercy [killing]."

Outside the court, she read out a further statement: "Seven years after my mother's death, my brothers, my sons and other members of the family were shocked and horrified to learn from the police that my mother, Mrs Betty Guy, may not have died from natural causes, and that my sister and her son were charged with murder. Over the past three years, the police have worked tirelessly to collect sufficient evidence to bring this to court. Now that the case has drawn to a close, we are satisfied that justice has prevailed and now we can close this very sad chapter in our lives."

The judge said Betty had been a "cheerful, lively and well-liked person". A friend, Mary Johnson, told the BBC, "We'd go away for the weekend and leave Betty in charge of the B&B [bed and breakfast] and the children. We'd come back and everything would be perfect. She was so, so good, very efficient and good with the kids. I could trust her with the children, no problem at all. I can't believe that anyone would hurt such a lovely, lovely person. She was a really kind, happy, jolly person."

The trial established the guilt of Penelope and Barry, but as is often the way with court trials, questions remained. For all the talk of a misguided mercy killing, why they murdered the 84-year-old remains a baffling poser. How premeditated was the murder? The "it's time, is it?" telephone conversation suggests mother and son had discussed and planned the killing beforehand. Were all the claims that Betty had cancer a bid by Penelope and Barry to dupe people like Rhianne into believing she was terminally ill, so that if and when they killed her they would have prepared false expectations of her demise? Was there an element of Penelope and Barry tiring of having to visit and support Betty?

Mother and son had suffered traumas in their pasts. Barry's father had beaten and abused Penelope and no doubt terrorised Barry, who then said he faced further damaging experiences as a soldier in Iraq. Had this contributed to their unconventional mother-son bond, one that was "unboundaried" – in Rhianne's apt phrase – and which made Betty and Rhianne uncomfortable? To some observers, the physicality and kissing might suggest an element of incest. Years later, Rhianne would say, "Looking back at it now, I would say that there was some kind of relationship other than mother and son going on."

Sandra Adams concurred. After the trial she said, "They would have conversations about sex, things most people would never discuss with their parents. It would make me feel very uncomfortable... There have been suggestions their relationship was sexual and it would not surprise me."

Somehow, in their rather unnatural co-dependency, had they egged each other on from fondness for Betty to murdering her?

Why had Barry gone on and on about having smothered his nan, revealing all to his ex-wife, ex-girlfriend, and even her sister and mother? Barry claimed this was all because of his need for attention, a craving he had because of his abusive father. Journalist Johanna Carr got a different impression. She said, "To me, it seemed either Barry was quite proud about what he had done and was boasting about it to his girlfriends, or a kinder view would be that he was quite remorseful and that was why he couldn't keep his mouth shut."

Dr Julian Boon, chartered forensic psychologist, also sensed an element of bragging. Of the exchanges recorded at Penelope's house by the police, he said, "The mother and the son, when they went back into the house, on bail, I think, couldn't get to the subject fast enough. He says something to the effect of, 'Don't worry about it, I was the one who did it,' which means, 'I want to have the notoriety for doing it. I killed someone.' And one thing you can know about the power-assertive character is that they commit their crimes – be they rape, arson, murder – but the one thing they can't do is let it rest there. They have to tell other people that they have done the crime." Power-assertive is a phrase often used to define serial offenders who need to express their aggression and dominance. The point here is that committing the murder was not enough; Barry wanted people to know about it.

Johanna Carr's view on the couple's motive was that even if, as the judge suggested, Barry and Penelope had acted from a misguided sense of mercy, "there is no evidence that Betty had ever asked them to do that, so rather it was something they had taken upon themselves, which they denied. Regardless, it was still murder…"

The most damning denunciation came, unsurprisingly, from Penelope and Barry's own relatives. His paternal grandmother, Margaret John, told the press that Barry had been convicted of armed robbery in his mid-teens for holding up a sweet shop in Haverfordwest with a knife. "There is something nasty and evil about him," she said. "I disowned him years ago. It could have been me. I will be glad to get him out of society, he is creepy."

Equally strong in her detestation was Debra John, Barry's aunt, who said after the trial, "They did it for kicks, they did it because they could do it and thought they could get away with it... they enjoyed killing her together. They are not mentally stable... It made me sick to see them in court together. They treated it like a big joke... they were making licking signs to each other."

The preceding account of events surrounding the murder of Betty Guy is based extensively on Rhianne Morris's interview with the *Murder by the Sea* programme. The reason for it being included in such depth is the courage she showed in reliving what for her was a painful, frightening time, and because of the insight her account gives into how someone, through no fault of their own and in a vulnerable period, can find themselves in a violent, abusive relationship.

The emotional fallout stayed with Rhianne long after she got away from Barry. She found she continued to be oppressed by preferences he had insisted on, and felt his baleful presence as she went about her life. "When I left Barry, I was still very much Barry's," she said. "I thought how Barry wanted me to. I did what Barry would have wanted me to do. And that lived with me for quite a while until I thought, *Actually, my life can't go on like this.*"

Cognitive behavioural therapy taught her to think for herself again, even in the most mundane situations. Where once she would be careful to make a cup of tea the way Barry liked it – teabag and milk in first – she now learned to follow her own choices again. "Me and my therapist, we managed to retrain my brain to think for me for a change, how I want it, what I want, what I want to do, rather than continuing to live the life that Barry wanted me to live.

"I don't feel like Barry's truly gone from my life, and I feel like he will always have a hold on me. I still hear his voice every now and again. There's a part of him that will always live with me – which makes me make decisions for the right reasons. I don't fall into the wrong situations anymore, but I do certainly still hear his voice. I have flashbacks. I still picture his face, but he doesn't have a hold on me. It's just a part of my life. It's always going to be there, unfortunately."

There has been a price to pay. She is not so quick to trust people now, but she feels stronger than she was back then. "It's very much opened my eyes to how much or how little you can know someone, regardless of how long you've been with them.

"I wouldn't necessarily call myself a role model, but what I would say is it doesn't matter who you are, where you are from, what family you have, what support network, you can just leave and you will be fine.

"Every day I think about the relationship I had with Barry and about what happened to Betty. Every day I thank my blessings that I didn't annoy him enough to push him that far over the edge. I definitely feel like I had a lucky escape.

"The more I knew, the more my own life was at risk. I'm lucky to be alive."

MITCHELL QUY

Southport

8

"She was a bright young girl, whole life ahead of her"

Southport, 1998
Victim: Lynsey Quy
Murderer: Mitchell Quy

Lynsey Quy was missing for 53 days before police were alerted in February 1999. Her husband, Mitchell, aged 24, told officers he had not seen his wife, a 21-year-old mother of two, since Christmas Day. She had, he said, walked out on him and the kids. He told police he had seen her being driven by a man through their home town of Southport in a dark Mercedes.

Her parents, Linda and Peter Wilson, were consumed with dread. They had heard nothing from Lynsey. Peter, who was 49, told the local newspaper, "Lynsey would never leave the children, because she was always with them and took them everywhere – she adores them."

Police issued an appeal for information. In the poster she was named as Lynsey Wilson Quy, five feet one inch tall, slim with dark hair, green eyes and freckles. There had been no other sightings of Lynsey since her husband said he had seen her on two occasions, once in the Mercedes and another time when he ran into her in a market. Mitchell Quy had appealed at a press conference for help in locating his wife. However, her whereabouts remained a complete mystery.

In April 1999, newly promoted Detective Superintendent Geoff Sloan, aged 45, settled down to his first task – reviewing the missing-from-home case of Lynsey Quy, a young former barmaid. Her tempestuous relationship with Mitchell would have been noted by the detective. Whatever hopes Lynsey may have had for the marriage were quickly sullied when she and Mitchell had a nasty argument on their wedding night.

At the time of her disappearance, she had been living at the family home with her husband and children, Robin, aged three, and 19-month-old Jack.

Det Supt Sloan also knew that the relationship had become so strained that Lynsey had, a short time before, sought help to get away from her husband. She had recently been living in a house provided by Sefton women's refuge, before getting back together with Mitchell – a decision she soon regretted. The detective said: "A social worker had not seen Lynsey for some time and decided that something wasn't right. She reported her missing and made the situation official. And that's how the missing-from-home inquiry began."

Once he had reviewed the case, Sloan decided this was more serious than a missing-person incident. He said, "As a result of that review, my findings were that Lynsey Quy had been murdered. A young mother wouldn't have left her children, certainly in the run-up to Christmas, and given the background of their relationship, I felt that it was a murder inquiry and that Mitchell Quy was the main suspect. On that basis, I went back to the chief officer group, gave them my findings, and they decided to upgrade the investigation to a murder inquiry. Subsequently, I was appointed as the Senior Investigating Officer."

Another factor that had made the detective suspicious was Quy's apparent enjoyment of being in the limelight. "He took part in a press conference in the initial stages," Sloan recalled. "I was of the opinion that he was overconfident, he was quite cocky. And in my experience, in lots of cases, the person who puts himself in front of the camera protesting their innocence, quite often is the guilty party."

It was important for Det Supt Geoff Sloan and his team to learn as much as possible about Quy and his relationship with Lynsey. She had been born in 1977, the youngest of six children. She got pregnant by her first serious boyfriend. An engagement followed, but Lynsey had second thoughts and called off the wedding. At five months pregnant and still only 17 years old, she met Mitchell Quy (the surname rhymes with "why"). Quy's parents, originally from Essex, had separated and his mother had died of cancer. He was not close to his father and did not have a particularly tight bond with his younger brother, Elliot. Sloan said, "He was quite chaotic in his work. He worked as a croupier, he worked at different venues." Within a week of meeting Lynsey, they were engaged. Five weeks after that, on 1 August 1995, they were wed.

"Even that day ended up with a big argument at the end of the night," Lynsey's father said, "so maybe that was a sign of things to come."

Robin, Lynsey's daughter by her former boyfriend, was born and Lynsey and Mitchell settled into their first flat, on Boundary Street, Southport. At first, Quy appeared to Lynsey's family and friends to be a nice guy. However, he soon showed his violent side.

"She wanted, I think, her own place, her own little family," Sloan said. "That was what she wished for, but it never materialised."

Her sister, Paula Houghton, recalled, "She wanted him out of the flat. I said, 'You've only just got married, give it a chance.' She said, 'You don't understand. He hits me.'"

A year after Robin was born, Lynsey was pregnant with Quy's child. The atmosphere at home, however, was so poison-ous that she decided she could not go through with the pregnancy and had an abortion. This would have been a particularly tough time for Lynsey, who was not having much contact with her family during this period. Quy walked out on her. After further attacks from him, Lynsey had taken out an injunction against her husband and was on her own for Christmas in 1996. She told her family he was sleeping with other women at this time.

LYNSEY WAS DEVOTED
TO HER TWO CHILDREN

After five months on her own, looking after Robin, Lynsey took her husband back in April 1997. She quickly became pregnant again. Meanwhile, Quy returned to his violent ways. When Lynsey was four months pregnant, he smashed up their Boundary Street home, trashing the furniture, smashing windows, breaking a door.

They were eventually evicted from their home but were together for Jack's birth in October 1997. But the reunited-violence-breakup cycle continued when they split again in April 1998. This time Women's Aid helped Lynsey to make a clean break from Quy, with assistance in finding a new home. She was also given a personal attack alarm. There is no question that the young mother was frightened of Quy. She told a friend he had a cool demeanour until he snapped. Even Quy himself said of the time he wrecked their Boundary Street accommodation, "I just lost the plot, went absolutely berserk, absolutely mental."

Sloan says, "She had quite a lot of conversations with close friends, and what she was always telling them was that she was afraid and that Mitchell had threatened her on the last occasion he'd left. He had said he was going to get someone to go round to beat her up. She was quite frightened about that. And, of course, at one stage he did go round and break into the house. So, while she never used the actual words that he was going to kill her, I think she was quite frightened of what he was capable of doing or what he was capable of getting someone else to do on his behalf."

Tragically, Lynsey gave Quy one last chance to get back into her life on Jack's first birthday in October 1998. "She didn't tell her mum or me or anyone else that she'd taken him back," her father said.

Quy would later say he wanted nothing from the marriage but to see his children. However, when Lynsey's sister visited on 22 October, she found Quy making himself aggressively at home. Sister Paula and Lynsey had been shopping, and Lynsey said she regretted his return and could not get him out of the house. Paula felt she could not help get him out, because when the family had intervened in the past there had been a lot of disagreements. Lynsey invited her into her place on this October evening. Paula found Quy drinking a can of lager. While she was there he stared her out: "If looks could kill, I'd have died on the spot." Lynsey hugged and kissed her sister, offering to give her her new phone number and slipping her a piece of paper. When Paula got home, she looked at the note and it read, "Please help me." The memory pained Paula. "I wish I could turn the clock back," she would say later.

In assessing the case, clinical forensic psychologist Professor Mike Berry highlighted the cycle of domestic abuse. "There were long periods where he left Lynsey with the children in the house while he went off and lived elsewhere," he said. "Then he would come back. This was the classic domestic-violence scenario – he leaves, he comes back, he's charming, everything would be hunky-dory for a few weeks." Then Quy would become sour and violent again.

Quy had succeeded in doing what many domestic abusers achieve – he cut Lynsey off from her loved ones. Forensic psychologist Dr Julian Boon was consulted by the police for an analysis of Quy during the investigation. "Tendencies to isolate a victim and tendencies towards coercive control are very indicative of someone who wants to have another totally kept in their world, and therefore exclude the other from anybody else's world," he said.

Lynsey loved Christmas and was looking forward to the season at the end of 1998. However, she had made an appointment with a solicitor to discuss getting a divorce. The appointment was for 16 December. Lynsey was last seen by someone other than her husband the day before that. She would not be reported missing until 5 February 1999. That would be done by the social worker who was concerned about her, not by her husband. Her mother phoned Lynsey on Christmas Eve to tell her the family had presents for the children – however, she could only leave a message for her daughter on the answer machine. Instead, Quy turned up in the rain that evening with the two children to collect the presents. He told the family that Lynsey was going out with her mates. He would later tell the police that she rolled in on Christmas morning "absolutely wrecked", and left him later that day. The family got no cards or presents from Lynsey.

So, according to Quy, Lynsey, who everyone agreed adored her children and took them everywhere with her, had missed Robin and Jack opening their presents on Christmas morning, and walked out with a strange man, without any explanation to her friends or family. This was drastically out of character for a woman who would "no more leave her children than fly through the air", in Dr Boon's vivid simile.

The police would form a different theory. Possibly on 16 December, before she could see the solicitor, Lynsey had had a bust-up with Quy and told him she was getting a divorce. In a rage, he had killed her and somehow disposed of her body.

GEOFF SLOAN, SENIOR INVESTIGATING OFFICER

Geoff Sloan recalled, "I was appointed SIO [senior investigating officer] and my main task then was to go back over the inquiry from start to finish and to make sure that every avenue, every inquiry had been undertaken, and to recheck that all the searches had been done properly, all the witnesses interviewed, and any other relevant information was looked at by us. Then we started the full murder inquiry."

Lynsey was missing for 18 months before the truth would emerge.

Loved ones making public appeals before television cameras for information about a missing family member will often appear to be reticent, afraid and worried. Mitchell Quy, on the other hand, took to the media circuit with the alacrity of a reality TV wannabe. He was in one of the initial press events in February 1999 to appeal for help in finding Lynsey. He would go on to appear on ITV's *This Morning* with Richard Madeley and Judy Finnigan, invite documentary makers into his home, and court the *Southport Visiter*, the local paper.

Introducing him in October 1999, six months after Lynsey was reported missing, Judy Finnigan said Quy was the only one who believed she was still alive. Why, she asked, did the police think he was a legitimate suspect in their murder inquiry? He replied, "Well, they say the husband's always the suspect."

Richard Madeley then asked, "Did you kill her?"

"No."

"Why would she walk out on the kids?"

"I don't know. That's a question you could only ask Lynsey."

During the 18-month police investigation, Quy claimed that when he spotted Lynsey in the dark Mercedes with another man, she had given him the V-sign. On the occasion he had bumped into her in the indoor market in Southport, he said she had called him names and sworn at him before walking away.

Det Supt Geoff Sloan's team did not believe any of this. "He gave these scenarios to try to convince people that Lynsey was still alive, was still in the area and was just flaunting herself to him," Sloan said. "And I think what he tried to do was make Lynsey the bad person in this. He was the good guy that had been abandoned with two children. He used the children as a shield."

When Dr Julian Boon began work on his analysis of Quy, he quickly spotted holes in Quy's account of Lynsey's disappearance. One of the first things that struck Boon was Quy's version of seeing his wife in the Mercedes. He said, "He made reference to the clothing of his wife and the so-called bloke who had come and taken her away in the black Mercedes. How could he have seen that? Immediately, the suspicion was raised. Then we move on to watching his behaviour as a suspect, where he was extraordinarily cocky, arrogant, everything about him screeches the behaviour of a psychopath, as in someone who truly does not care or has any guilt for anything that they do, and that they manipulate and totally control people and events thereafter."

Quy became bolder with his media appearances. He called in a local reporter to say he was suing the police for victimising him. When asked by another reporter, whom he allowed into his home with a film crew, whether he killed Lynsey, Quy at first called the question stupid. When the question was repeated, he gave the chilling reply, "Wait and find out." He cannot help but smile a bit as he says it.

The senior investigator began to wonder why Quy had started to wear glasses during his media appearances. He had worn them at his wedding, but in general he did not. "It was when he started to perform in front of the TV that he wore these glasses," Det Supt Sloan said. "I wondered what that was about. During the course of looking at the different films or programmes he'd made, we came to the conclusion that he was wearing these spectacles to give himself some sort of gravitas, to make him look a bit more intelligent. And actually, my professional opinion was to hide his eyes from the camera. I felt he was hiding behind those glasses."

The trouble for Quy was that nobody believed him. The police, journalists, Lynsey's family, right down to the local newsagent, all sensed that he was a liar. What he was saying about his wife was so out of character for her. Friends and family often commented on her love and devotion to her children. She took them everywhere, walking for miles with them in their double buggy. Her mother, Linda, said, "She looked after them really well. Mitchell was never there for the children. It's upsetting when she [Robin] says, 'I can't find me mummy. Can you help me find me mummy?'"

In addition, no one – apart from number-one suspect Mitchell Quy – claimed to have seen Lynsey alive after 15 December 1998. "I employed a forensic psychologist [Dr Boon] to view the films, to look at the newspaper articles," Sloan said. "Both of us determined that Quy was an egotist and a self-publicist. He was denying the inevitable."

During the investigation, Quy tried several times to meet the senior investigating officer. "I decided from the beginning that I wouldn't meet Mitchell Quy," Det Supt Sloan said. "In my opinion, he was caught in the media. He'd been on with Richard and Judy. He had undertaken other programmes. The *Southport Visiter* were regularly visiting him, and he was coming out with different quotes and really lambasting the police inquiry. My main concern was to concentrate my efforts on trying to find the evidence which would convict him. So my view was that I would not meet him until the end of the inquiry."

A sign of how the inquiry and distress over Lynsey's disappearance had become a game to Quy came when he started taunting the senior investigator. Over Christmas

1999, Quy sent a card to Sloan with a gift, some hair dye for men. The joke was that Sloan was under so much pressure, he was going grey. Such a prank may have got a laugh from Quy's mates, but it was hardly the act of a concerned husband hoping the police would locate his missing wife.

For Dr Julian Boon, this also was a strong indicator of psychopathy. "Psychopathic humour is of a rarefied world, a community kept to psychopaths," he said. "And it's pretty difficult to spot if you're not someone who really understands psychopathy. The classic example would be a serial killer who dumps a body on the side of a road, but dumps it below a sign which says, 'No Dumping'. Right away your alarm bells are ringing because you know jolly well that they are likely to be psychopathic. In his case, Quy really, really blew it in terms of any doubt that he was psychopathic when he sent hair dye to the senior investigating officer, saying, 'This will give you confidence.'" It was a typical prank of an arrogant, psychopathic personality.

DR JULIAN BOON

Quy was also not above taunting Lynsey's dad. Peter Wilson had the painful task of going to his son-in-law's home during these months of dread for the family to collect the children while the search for Lynsey continued. He turned down Quy's invitations to come inside, preferring to wait on the doorstep. Quy told a television reporter, "I couldn't walk up to the front door and face the person I thought killed my daughter… I admire the guy in a way."

Dr Boon felt Quy relished the chance to torment Lynsey's family. "It's entirely conceivable that he derived some benefit from Lynsey's family being highly distressed. Her father made absolutely no secret of the fact that he didn't like Quy. When Lynsey's sister went into the house, she was made to feel as unwelcome as possible, with him staring at her without saying a single word until she decided she just had to leave. His mother said she also felt extremely unwelcome whenever he was around. So, one can only think that he got some external derivative pleasure by isolating Lynsey, and, therefore, if you do that, well, the next step is once she's missing you can get off on seeing the family unhappy."

In August 1999, Quy was sentenced to community service by Southport magistrates after he admitted forging cheques in his wife's name and cashing her benefits. His justification was that he needed the money for the children, but in an ITV documentary he said he was "cashing cheques out of Lynsey's account, claiming income support, which I was entitled to anyway, it just wasn't in my name". Again, Quy wanted to be seen as a victim. On arrival at court, a demonstration organised by Lynsey's family greeted him.

Nevertheless, Quy seemed to revel in being the focus of the turmoil. "I think it worked for him on a number of levels," Dr Boon said. "First of all, he could quite literally get away with murder all the time that the body was not discovered. Secondly, I think it worked for him where he absolutely loved being the centre of attention. Thirdly, and this, I reckon, must be incontestable, that he enjoyed pulling the tail of the police and saying to them, you're no closer to getting me now. And also, there's an element of duping delight. He gets a sense of power, in my opinion, by duping the police into making them go off all over the place looking for the phantom Lynsey that he knew full well was dead."

Quy's criticisms of the police, though brushed aside as a ploy and a bid for attention by detectives, was just one of several pressures bearing down on the investigation. The case was covered in the national press and television as police searched the couple's home three times, examined waterways and sewers, and excavated open ground around Southport. Various mediums and even self-proclaimed psychic Uri Geller chipped in with tips on where Lynsey's body might be found. Det Supt Sloan also had a duty to Lynsey's family, keeping them informed and reassured that every effort was being made to bring the case to a conclusion. The family was under considerable strain during these months. They bought a minibus to carry relatives to sites around Merseyside to search for Lynsey at weekends. They were tormented by fear of never finding out where she was, in addition to the parallel dread that something awful had happened to her.

Police found no forensic evidence at the couple's house. By managing to keep Lynsey's disappearance secret for 53 days, Quy gave himself plenty of time to obliterate traces of the killing. "We did determine he'd bought huge quantities of bleach around the time that Lynsey disappeared," Det Supt Sloan said. "My opinion was that he'd used that bleach to clean the house thoroughly, and during the course of the documentary he was making [filmed by ITV], you could see quite clearly he was cleaning and decorating the house."

"There can be little doubt that after 18 months, he really thought he would get away with it," Dr Boon said. As long as no body was discovered, Quy probably believed he was untouchable.

Another hurdle for detectives was that it was difficult to prosecute a murder case if the victim's body could not be located. Det Supt Sloan said, "If you haven't got a body, it's very, very difficult because if you do charge somebody and it goes before a jury, it's a huge issue for a jury to determine a person's guilt of murder without that physical evidence. So, while I was always certain that Mitchell had killed Lynsey, the fact that we didn't have a body was uppermost in my mind. Are we going to be able to charge him at the end of the day? And if we do, are we able to convince a jury that he actually killed her in the absence of a body?" The priority became to build a solid enough circumstantial case to convince the Crown Prosecution Service to charge Quy without Lynsey's remains.

To do that, it was crucial for the investigation to demonstrate that Lynsey was not alive, that there was no trace of her anywhere throughout the whole country. Sloan explained, "There were no traces at airports or stations. No reports of her visiting hospitals or dentists or anything."

Detectives discovered that before she vanished, Lynsey had visited a local dentist with a severe pain. Root canal work was needed and a temporary filling had been fitted until that could be done. Having contacted every dental practice in the UK via the NHS, the detectives learned she had not sought to have that painful condition treated. She also never turned up for the solicitor's appointment to discuss a divorce, or a hairdresser's booking to get her hair styled for Christmas. Her mother said she had not applied for a passport and had even left her bank card behind.

"The other issues were that she'd made little lists and notes of Christmas presents and trinkets that she'd bought for the children," Sloan said. "We found those. She'd made diary entries about how dire the relationship was. My own view and those of officers – particularly women and mothers – who were on the inquiry was that no mother would leave the children to a person she detested in the run-up to Christmas. Nobody would do that."

Mitchell Quy was arrested on suspicion of murder on 7 June 2000, 18 months after Lynsey's disappearance. In a bid to take him out of his comfort zone, it was decided to convey him to a police station he was not familiar with, rather than Southport. He would also be questioned about different phases of the investigation rather than in a chronological order, to throw him off any practised responses. For his first 36 hours in custody, he refused to answer questions.

Det Supt Sloan said, "Throughout the investigation, Mitchell was cocky and an egotist, and he absolutely loved all the attention he was getting. He denied everything that had happened. And my view was that once we'd got permission from the Crown Prosecution Service to charge him with murder, despite the fact that we didn't have a body, I thought that would come as a shock to him. At no stage did he think that we would charge him."

The police sensed that Quy was starting to feel uncomfortable with the questions put to him. Sloan then went in to meet the suspect for the first time. If Quy thought this might be an opportunity for grandstanding or further fun and games, the senior investigator put him straight immediately. Sloan refused Quy's offer to shake hands and told him he was going to charge him with murder. He added that he would also charge his brother, Elliot, with various offences. Quy was charged with Lynsey's murder on the evening of 8 June.

John Davies was one of the custody officers at Copy Lane police station in Bootle, near Liverpool, where Quy was detained. It was Davies's job to ensure Quy was treated in accordance with all regulations, including giving the prisoner access to the exercise yard. "Mitchell Quy didn't act like somebody who was concerned," Davies recalled. "I wouldn't have been that calm in his situation."

It fell to Davies to formally charge and refuse bail to Quy. "He was allowed to go to a consultation room with his solicitor," Davies said. "After a short while, a message was received over the intercom: Quy wanted to speak to me. I went to the interview room and was told by a solicitor that Quy had something to show me, at which point he produced a piece of paper with a pencil drawing, a diagram of the area around by Southport Zoo. And on that piece of paper, there were indications of where body parts may be found. At this point, I obtained a forensic bag and asked Quy to place the piece of paper in that bag."

As Quy was being driven from Copy Lane to Southport, he turned to the officer who had handcuffed him, Steve Molyneux, and asked for a cigarette. An officer in the escort gave him one. "He was calm," Molyneux recalled. "Then out the blue on that journey he admitted that he'd murdered Lynsey, and he would like to show us where the body parts were located. There were no tears, no real emotion. It was just very calm and he sort of just bowed his head." The officer recorded this stunning admission in his notebook and made a statement when they reached Southport, which was given to CID. Molyneux's view of Quy's abrupt confession was, "I think it came to the time where he thought, *I can't continue this charade any longer.*"

Senior investigator Sloan recalled what happened next: "I got a phone call from the sergeant to say that he had admitted to killing Lynsey." Quy revealed that he had dismembered her body and had even drawn his map. "He was prepared to show us with this diagram where he'd put the body parts. We were absolutely horrified, because never at any stage had I considered that to be the case."

His reflection on why Quy caved in when faced with the reality of the murder charge went a little further than Molyneux's: "I think he considered that the first chapter of this episode had finished," Sloan said. "And in order to continue his notoriety and the attention that he was getting, he decided to confess and continue with his story. He was basically just an egotist, and he wanted to continue the story, to start another chapter. I don't think he showed any remorse whatsoever. Never has done. He wanted the notoriety."

Sloan's estimation of Quy solidified when the murderer took officers to the sites where he had disposed of his wife's body parts. "He looked around and asked if the press were there. He was quite eager to be seen on camera. He was laughing and joking with the officers." Quy showed them exactly where he had hidden her "carcass", as he put it.

He had chosen sites he was familiar with – near the go-cart establishment where he used to work, and the railway embankment at the bottom of a road where he once lived. During the recovery work, police found Lynsey's trunk and arms on ground to the rear of the go-kart track. At the railway embankment, Quy showed police where he left her legs. Her head and hands were never found. The body parts were tightly sealed in bin bag-type wrappings, which made securing DNA to identify Lynsey fairly straightforward.

Police believed Quy had put Lynsey's body in a suitcase and then ordered a taxi to transport it.

An indication of Quy's total absence of feelings as he did this was that he took the children with him. Sloan said, "When Mitchell was disposing of the various body parts he always had the children with him. He wouldn't be able to leave them with anyone else. So, when he got the taxi to take what he described as Lynsey's torso to the back of the go-cart premises, the children, from his account, were with him. Similarly, they were in the pram at the embankment, where he deposited the two legs separately. So he used the children as a shield for it.

When it came to the actual murder, the theory was that Lynsey may have confronted her husband over the stolen benefit cheque. If, during the argument, she said she would be divorcing him, this may have tipped Quy into one of his violent rages. Lynsey was petite and had trusted him in the past, but this show of determination from her may have been too much for an abuser such as Quy, who always sought to intimidate and control his wife. If she really broke free of the marriage, his powerbase in the household and grip over her would be gone.

"He couldn't control his emotions," Sloan said. "I believe that he killed her in that moment of pique. Then he decided to bluff it out. He told us it had happened in the living room, that he strangled her for some time before she was dead. Then he removed her upstairs to a double bed and placed clothing and blankets over her to conceal the body from the children."

Sloan and Dr Boon both did not trust Quy's version of events. "I personally believe it was a fit of rage," the forensic psychologist said. "But did it happen in the way he said it? There I am dubious, to say the least. He says he held her neck for 20 minutes. That is unusual. Now that can be for two reasons. One, that he has true hatred for her, for defying him and saying, I want to divorce, get out of my life. But equally possible is that he's trying to show that he had lost all control... was in a state of horror about what he'd done."

He adds that Quy did turn on the tears during his police interview. These "crocodile tears" and the suggestion that he lost control, Dr Boon suggests, were probably a bid by Quy to avoid the appearance of being a callous, premeditated killer at any impending trial, thereby hoping to reduce his sentence. Dr Boon said, "That's sheer psychopathy. Go with the cushier route, put on the tears and then go do your porridge and you'll get a shorter sentence." The normal reaction of someone who had killed in a fit of anger would be to call the police – *My god, my god, what have I done?* Whether or not Quy was trying to manipulate events so that he might get a lighter sentence, his subsequent actions gave him away. He and Elliot disposed of Lynsey, and Quy spent 18 months denigrating her reputation and playing mind games with the police and public.

Dr Boon never interviewed Quy, but based his assessment of him on police reports and tapes. "If indeed he was a psychopath, he would want some kind of revenge for anybody daring, *daring*, to treat him without full and due respect." Lynsey's bid to divorce him would have been seen as such a challenge by Quy.

"It was he," Dr Boon stated, "who said to camera [in a TV report], 'Do I look like a psychopath?' Supercilious smile. 'Who knows what a psychopath looks like?' Supercilious smile. My answer is, 'You do.'"

After the killing, Quy bathed the children and put them to bed. The body was at some point put in the loft. As part of his confession, Quy revealed his brother's role in what happened next. He recruited Elliot to help him dispose of the body. "I think Elliot purchased the knife, quite a sharp, big knife," said Sloan. "And when the children were asleep in bed, the two men brought the body down into the bath and, over a period of time, dissected the body."

Elliot looked up to Mitchell and was easily led by him. Quy said his brother had taken the head and hands of Lynsey in a black bin bag, walked down the road, and put them in a bin. Sloan doubts this. "I felt that there was a blunt-force instrument used towards Lynsey's face or head. And I think the hands as well, because quite conceivably they would have had defensive marks." So, it is possible that Quy's attack on his wife was more vicious that he stated, and to hide this fact he disposed of her head and hands in such a way that they would never be located.

Prof Mike Berry felt the dissection might give a different insight into Quy's motivation. "By his own definition, he took two days to chop up the body," he said. "What I find interesting is that his younger brother, Elliot, was supposed to have had some butchery skills. So you would have thought that between the two of them they could have cut up the body much quicker. Does that suggest he actually took pleasure in taking her apart? The fact that he took the head off, again, I think is interesting because I think it shows he really did want to destroy her. That shows a great deal of anger and hatred towards her."

On 16 January 2001, Mitchell Quy was found guilty at Liverpool Crown Court of Lynsey's murder and jailed for life. Having initially admitted manslaughter, he subsequently changed his plea to guilty. Elliot pleaded guilty to helping to dispose of the body and received a seven-year sentence.

Mr Justice Brian Leveson QC said in passing sentence on Mitchell Quy that he had, after murdering and disposing of Lynsey, embarked over 18 months on a "deception of breathtaking cynicism, appearing on the television bemoaning your wife's absence and castigating police for directing their attentions towards you... The callous disregard which you demonstrated towards your children, in particular Robin, who you caused to believe had been abandoned by their mother, can only be characterised as evil."

Dr Julian Boon summed up the abusive husband's exposure for his vile crime: "Like so many murderers before him, [Quy was] a man whose conviction was secured by him being consumed by his own vanity."

Quy has been in prison for the past two decades. Psychiatric nurse turned author Chris Kinealy encountered Quy early on in Altcourse Prison. He gave interesting insights into the killer once he was out of the public limelight.

Quy had been remanded on the vulnerable prisoners' wing because of the brutality of his crime and, said Kinealy, his "unpleasant personality. He was extremely unpopular with the ordinary inmates. It really does take something, in a category A maximum security prison, to get treated as a pariah by the other prisoners, and he managed this." Quy approached Kinealy and said, "All right, mate?" This was an immediate break with prison protocol, where officials are addressed as Guv, Doc or Boss. Quy asked if Kinealy knew what he was in for. Kinealy did know but denied it. This was to avoid feeding Quy any sense of importance or celebrity status. The two men talked and Quy discussed his crime, even making a sick joke about it.

"He came across to me as a clinical psychopath, aggressive, very grandiose, delusions of grandeur, inflated self-worth," was Kinealy's assessment. "He really thought he was someone special. And even without the murder, he would have been like that. He showed no feeling inside, or foresight. He had this inflated ego, seemed to think he'd done something incredibly clever, he was a celebrity, waiting for people to recognise his greatness and, by and large, he was an extremely unpleasant, psychopathic young man."

Kinealy got to see what happened when that inflated sense of self-importance was punctured. He said, "The only time I saw him display any emotion was the day of the sentence. He got life imprisonment with a recommended minimum of 17 years. He came and told me this through the steel grille. As I was leaving, he stopped me and said, 'What happens to me now?' I said, 'Well, now you'll be sent to a long-stay high-security prison,' as opposed to Altcourse, which was a disbursal prison. A lot of people come in for very short sentences or alternatively, just on remand. Once he'd been sentenced, he would have been shipped to a long-stay prison. And I said, 'When you get there, you'll have plenty of time to settle in.'

"So, a couple of days later, he took an overdose. He was actually on, I believe it was, amitriptyline, which is an anti-depressant. He secreted these tablets on his person, saved them up and took an overdose. I think what he felt was an overwhelming sense of disappointment. He was the celebrity who just got 17 years. Truthfully, I don't know what he expected to happen – that he was going to be treated as the celebrity he thought he was? When he wasn't and he'd had a couple of days to think about it, he went and took his overdose. It wasn't fatal. Obviously, he lived."

What stayed with Kinealy was Quy's utter lack of feeling for Lynsey and what he had done to her. "If a normal person kills somebody accidentally in a traffic accident, whatever, they would be devastated," he said. "They'd be upset, in floods of tears, they'd go to church, light a candle, whatever. In his case, he just thought it was all a huge joke.

"Psychopaths classically always laugh at bad news, whether the bad news is about a friend or someone who they hate. They don't have any real friends." This reflects Dr Boon's remarks above about psychopathic humour and how it targets the perceived misfortunes of other people.

Putting Quy behind bars still stands out for retired senior investigating officer Geoff Sloan. "The enduring memory I've got of this case is the brutality of it. A young mother cut short in her life, leaving two young children to grow up without a mother. She was a bright young girl, whole life ahead of her. She clearly got in the wrong relationship with Mitchell. It's just a sad situation, never getting the whole of the body back so that her family could put her to rest in peace."

Lynsey Wilson was a young woman who had the tragic misfortune to think that she could build a life and family with Mitchell Quy, a man it is unlikely could form a mutually happy relationship with anyone. The speed with which he wooed and wed a pregnant and perhaps vulnerable Lynsey was suspiciously hasty. No doubt he saw her as someone he could control and dominate. The nice guy immediately dissolved into a violent, controlling, isolating aggressor. The Office of National Statistics published figures, based on 10 years of data, showing that in the year ending March 2016, 1.2 million women reported being victims of domestic abuse in England and Wales. The report also stated that two women a week are murdered by a partner or former partner. The case of Lynsey Wilson gives some insight into the human damage and ongoing feelings of loss and regret that lie buried in the statistics.

The torment for her family has been desolating. Lynsey's sister Paula Houghton said of Quy, "I hate him. Does he not have any feeling for what he's done to that young girl, who had no one in the end? She was just a lonely girl with two children. And I have to sit here with my guilt for not being there for her – so does the rest of the family."

Peter Wilson, Lynsey's brother, who was 21 years old when she was murdered, never got over losing her. He told his father, "There is no point in living. I may as well join Lynsey." In 2001, Peter hanged himself at the family home in Southport.

MALCOLM GREEN

St Brides

9

"This guy is going to kill somebody one day"

Cardiff, 1971, and Bristol, 1990
Victims: Glenys Johnson, Clive Tully
Murderer: Malcolm Green

Clive Tully, a 24-year-old backpacking New Zealander, was missing. The trouble was, no one knew it.

He had originally pitched up in Newport, Wales, largely thanks to his cousin, David Tully. "I'd gone out to New Zealand on a working holiday," David said. "I was able to track the family down because his [Clive's] father had moved to New Zealand from the UK in the 50s, when I was quite small."

All David and his family in Wales knew was that they had relatives somewhere in Auckland. David made his trip down under in the 1970s. He found work in Wellington and while there was invited to go up to Auckland with a friend for a long weekend. He recalled, "Out of curiosity, I went to the GPO [General Post Office] in Wellington, looked up people with my surname in the telephone book. There weren't many, only two or three. And the first one I picked turned out to be Clive's mother. What I've found out recently was that even though I was only there for a few hours, all the kids could remember me from that time, and X number of years later, when Clive had grown up, he decided that he wanted to come to the UK on a working holiday and meet as many of the family as he could."

And Clive had done that, visiting family members in the Newport area, from where his father, Joseph, had emigrated decades before. He was also able to follow the All Blacks rugby union side during their tour that year, which included a fixture in Newport. David remembered his cousin as being a reserved young man. "The time that he was in Newport," David said, "I think it was the first time he'd been out of New Zealand, so maybe he was a little bit apprehensive about what his future would be. But I think he was like most of the family, relatively quiet. You know, there wasn't anything nasty about him. He was just Clive."

Clive's recent movements had been as follows. After meeting the Newport relatives, he had taken some building work in Bristol for a firm owned by a family called Higgins. As part of the job, Clive could use a flat owned by his employer in Luxton Street, Bristol. There, on 16 October 1989, he met and became friends with another tenant and Higgins employee, a 44-year-old man called Malcolm Green. However, Clive's job had turned sour. His boss, Michael Higgins, said the New Zealander had walked out on the job when he had not received a Christmas bonus. He was subsequently sacked.

The sunshine of Spain and Portugal then proved an attractive option for the young man, and Clive spent the early months of 1990 visiting those countries. He returned to

Bristol on 11 March, having run out of money. One of the last people to see Clive alive was a man called Dennis Coombs, who had given the young traveller £200 to buy a flight back to the UK. Coombs said Clive had stayed with him in Bristol for five days while looking for work.

Clive had asked an uncle in Bristol if he could stay with him, but having been turned down he ended up seeking out his mate Malcolm Green, or Mack, as he was known. On 17 March he turned up at the home of Green's girlfriend and asked if he could crash with Green back in Luxton Street. The older man agreed, took him round to Luxton Street and then returned to his girlfriend.

Backpacking could be a precarious way to see the world, and in time-honoured fashion Clive was making friends and was grateful for any hospitality, no doubt willing to return the favour should any of his Good Samaritans find themselves in New Zealand one day. The peril for Clive – one that he clearly did not foresee, and that his instincts had not alerted him to – was that Malcolm Green was not a Good Samaritan. He was just about the last person in Bristol from whom he should have accepted hospitality. It is most unlikely Clive knew that Green was on parole from prison when they met, and certain that he was unaware his mate had just served nearly 18 years for the depraved mutilation and murder of a woman.

At this point, Clive's relatives were not sure where he was, other than that he had gone to Bristol. Some no doubt assumed he would be heading home from there in the near future. His family in Auckland did not know where he was either – only that he was probably somewhere in the UK.

Malcolm Green returned to the Luxton Street flat on 19 March. Clive Tully was never seen alive again.

Malcolm John Green was born in Cardiff on 31 January 1947. He was the fifth of 12 children. He was brought up in Ely in the Welsh capital, educated at a secondary modern school and spent time in borstal.

It was at around the age of 12 that he suffered a horrific experience. He and his younger brother were playing on a railway line when his sibling was hit and decapitated by a train. What must have compounded this trauma was that Malcolm Green was then selected to identify his dead brother at the morgue. Why a child would be chosen for this grisly task is beyond comprehension.

Journalists like to claim that this episode sparked a bloodlust in Green, but he did not speak about this disturbing experience, so it is difficult to know precisely what impact it had. There is, however, the possibility that he felt some guilt and shame as a child that he had not prevented the death. Could this have fuelled the anger that later dominated his controlling, violent nature?

Clinical forensic psychologist Professor Mike Berry feels sure the railway tragedy was a turning point for Green. "That is a tremendously stressful occurrence in anybody's life," he said, "but at the age of 12 it would obviously have a long-term effect on him. Now, whether he was involved in his brother's death or not, we can only speculate, but clearly he had problems from that age onwards. When he left school he went to work in a slaughterhouse and clearly enjoyed cutting up animals as part of his job. He carried on doing that for a number of years, and then at the age of 24 he went to work as a crane operator. So, has he at that point lost the opportunity to express his anger by cutting up animals?"

He certainly grew up to be handy with his fists, his body battered by the many fights he got into as a young man. He married in his early twenties and lived in Coed-y-Gores, Llanedeyrn, with his wife, Marilyn Stephenson. In 1991 she described him: "Some of the time he was polite and charming, attractive to women and highly sexed. At other times he could be violently possessive, fanatically tidy, and subject to fits."

Marilyn said when Green suffered his "fits" he would go into convulsions and had to be held down until he blacked out. "Most of the furniture was ruined by him," she said. "He threw me across the room.

"He'd been in a lot of fights, he knew how to look after himself. A doctor at Cardiff jail said he was so covered in scars that if you pulled one stitch he'd unravel."

Green was controlling and overbearing. He once said to Marilyn that he wondered what it would be like to kill someone. This was likely all part of his need to intimidate her with fear.

He struggled to stick at one job, moving from work as a salesman to his roles as slaughterhouse butcher and crane operator.

In June 1971 his wife was pregnant but suffered a miscarriage. It is hard not to wonder if the pregnancy presented some threat to Green's tidy, controlled world, because his behaviour now veered from reckless to homicidal.

Gordon Shumack was a young temporary detective who encountered Green at this time, immediately sensing a poisonous character. He said, "I was working night duty when we had a call that an alarm had gone off at the butcher shop in Bridge Street, Cardiff, which was a Jewish butcher's – whereby they only sold kosher products – and there were live chickens in the back yard of this place. The alarm had been set off by broken glass from the front door and there was blood at the scene. So, in Sherlock Holmes style, I followed the trail of blood to his [Green's] house, arrested him and brought him back to the station."

In those days there was no technology that could examine the blood evidence quickly. It had to be sent to the Forensic Science Laboratory to be analysed against a sample of his blood. This could take up to a month.

"In the meantime," Shumack said, "you couldn't keep somebody in custody whilst that test was being done. So he was released on Section 38 police bail."

Shumack found Green to have a disconcerting presence. "It's a very long time ago, but it's not very often you meet someone where you think, *This guy is going to kill somebody one day*," he said. "It's only really happened to me in my career a couple of times when you've got that thing about a person that you're speaking with, or interviewing, that one day in the future this man or woman is going to cause some serious harm.

"It was the coldness of him, his eyes and the way he spoke. He was totally detached, seemed to me to have no emotion, and it was just strange. When you speak to people, you can usually understand whether they are happy or sad or whatever. And later on, you get to learn to read people's body language. But this guy was just stone cold. No emotion. And you can't describe it any other way than to say he had strange eyes."

The young detective did not have to wait long until his instinct that Green would do "serious harm" was proved correct. While Marilyn was in hospital recovering from her miscarriage on 21 June, Green – clearly not that distressed by his wife being unwell – decided to go clubbing. Up to this time, Green's actions had been a scattergun of reckless, vicious self-indulgence – fighting, burgling a shop, and repeatedly stabbing a life-size dummy at home. And these are just the behaviours we know about.

That June night, he took his appetite for violence to a new, depraved extreme. He encountered a woman during his carousing, Glenys Johnson, aged 40. She was from Grangetown, a domestic cleaner who may have also sold sex. The encounter likely took place in Cardiff's docks area, which in 1971 was unrecognisable from the leisure and cultural centre it has been transformed into in the years since. During the Industrial Revolution, Cardiff was one of the world's key ports, a Mecca of shipping, iron and coal. It used to be said there were once so many ships packed into port you could walk from one side of the docks to the other by leaping from one vessel to the next. Where today there are bistros, luxury flats, hotels and, of course, the Millennium Centre, there were warehouses, cranes and rough sailor's pubs. The 1970s were the last gasp of the docks' industrial strength, the final exports of coal from the valleys having ceased in 1964.

Gordon Shumack remembers the area, and its sex trade. "The way that the girls work today is different to years ago," he said. "In those days there was quite a lot of them, and they used to meet in the Custom House pub on Bute Street. The landlord there, a guy called Johnny Lord, was very welcoming to them. And one of the ladies was more or less their shop steward. So, if something had happened whereby they were concerned, Pam would speak for the rest of them and voice their concerns.

"But it was a very dangerous occupation. We used to have part-timers, where they would be working in an office and slip out in the lunchtime and do a bit of business and go back to work. But the regular girls, everybody knew them all. We had a small vice squad in those days who were charged with looking after them, and they got arrested from time to time because they had committed an offence. But it was a dangerous occupation. The back of what are now apartment buildings, like Edward England Potato Warehouse, round the back of each canal wharf, there were derelict warehouses where they would go and ply their trade, or they'd get into a car with a punter and drive into one of these yards. That was quite open, and they would then have sex in the car."

A trial at Cardiff Assizes would later hear that Glenys Johnson was "brutally and viciously murdered" on wasteland in Wharf Street. The woman's throat received a deep, five-inch cut, her abdomen was slashed, and she had 20 stab wounds. Her body was left under a car.

The attack was a spur-of-the-moment explosion by Green. Prof Berry pointed out, "What was interesting was that he didn't use a knife. He used a piece of glass. So, when he met his victim, he wasn't armed with a knife. Again, it gives an indication of impulsivity, that he hadn't planned to kill his victim, but for whatever reason, he did and then cut her up with glass."

Mark Waters was a detective chief superintendent who would be in a charge of building a second case against Green later in 1990 in connection with Clive Tully's disappearance.

MARK WATERS,
FORMER HEAD
OF GWENT CID

But he was familiar with the case file for the murder of Glenys Johnson, and he explained the difficulties investigators faced in 1971. "She was found and she'd been cut quite badly," he said. "I was told that she had cut marks on her stomach and her throat had been cut and her head virtually severed – a very strange murder. On the face of it, it looked as though they were never going to get anywhere. Where do you start? And they really didn't have anything until they started getting phone calls."

Post-mortem mutilation is called overkill by criminal psychologists, and often signifies an attempt by the attacker to obliterate their victim. This was not enough for Glenys Johnson's killer. He also wanted to taunt the police about what he had done.

The anonymous phone caller to local police said: "Have you found the body yet? There will be four more." The caller returned to the same phone box near Cardiff docks at least twice.

These calls were quickly traced to a phone box near the steel works. Mark Waters related what happened next: "Officers raced down there and a man was just leaving the telephone box. They took hold of him, arrested him, basically, and he said, 'I haven't done anything, I just called my wife.' They said, 'We know you just rang us.' He said, 'No, I didn't ring, but I know who was in there before me. It was a chap who I work with in the steelworks, a chap called Green. He was there before me – I followed him into the box.' And they then arrested Green."

After the murder, Green had apparently gone into his workplace, at the British Steel Corporation East Moors works, where he was employed as a crane operator, and used the shower to wash his bloodstained clothing.

On being arrested, he initially admitted his guilt. He said, "I started walking home by myself. I had had a lot to drink and wanted to sober up. At the bottom of Bute Street I was approached by this woman. She asked me if I was interested in business. She started screaming and pulling my clothes. I lost my temper and exploded. The next thing I remember was walking home."

He apparently also said something about only having a "comb and a shilling". Had he haggled with Glenys Johnson over a price? If he was drunk and there was any disagreement, his anger could have sent him into a violent outburst.

Green retracted his admission of guilt at the subsequent trial, claiming the comments above were made up by the police. He also said he had "no idea" how his victim's blood ended up on his shoes, or how his blood came to be on her clothing. It was not much of a defence.

When police searched his home after arresting Green, they found a dummy wrapped in carpet that had been stabbed repeatedly. A knife was sticking out of its neck.

On 5 November 1971 Green was found guilty of Glenys Johnson's murder and given a minimum 25-year prison term. "I'll appeal against this," he shouted as he was led from the dock.

Green clearly imagined himself as some kind of 1970s Jack the Ripper. The taunting phone messages to the police were similar to the 1888 letter to the Central News Agency, which was forwarded to Scotland Yard, purporting to be from "Jack the Ripper". Green's phone call bragging that "there will be four more" and the stabbed dummy suggests that he had been fantasising about murder with a blade. The irony is that if he had not made the phone calls to the police, he could well have got away with the crime. Mark Waters was in no doubt that Green's phone taunts were a major blunder.

His wife Marilyn would later reflect on how lucky she had been to have escaped the marriage with her life. While he was in prison, she unsurprisingly left Green, and the couple were divorced during the 1980s.

Malcolm Green was sent to Gartree Prison in Leicestershire. "He was a very troublesome prisoner," said William Glynn, a former detective chief inspector. "He was involved in the Gartree riots, and he was never a very co-operative prisoner." For much of his time behind bars, Green was belligerent and aggressive.

It would, however, appear that Green learned how to play the system. By the late 1980s he was in his 40s and was keeping his head down. He was eventually allowed out on day release, attended a technical college and studied A-level biology. He met a woman who became his girlfriend. Everything about his performance of good behaviour can be seen in retrospect as a bid to convince the parole board that he was no threat to the public and safe to release.

Prof Berry said, "Twenty years is a long time to spend in prison on a life sentence, so the authorities must have had some reservations about him." But did he eventually realise that aggression and troublemaking were not in his best interests if he ever wanted to get out again? "He could have easily lied about his impulses," Prof Berry said. "If people don't know he's fantasising about killing, about cutting up people and animals, he doesn't tell anybody and builds up trust and relationships with a therapist in the prison system, then he can get through."

Even without the benefit of hindsight, however, the decision to release Green seems lax. His murder of Glenys Johnson had been extraordinarily violent. At the time he had said he would kill four more victims. He may have subsequently passed this off as insincere bragging, but the evidence of the dummy he had been hacking at should surely have suggested to the prison psychiatrists that he had a dangerous fixation on stabbing and murder. Green had hardly been a model prisoner, even if he had been on his best behaviour after many years of aggression and hostility. He might have been eligible for release in 1983 but had tried to escape and been committed to a further six years' imprisonment.

In the event, he served almost 18 years and was released from Leyhill Open Prison in Gloucestershire on parole on 16 October 1989. He was 44 years old. Seeking a new start, he settled in Bristol.

Five months later, Clive Tully had vanished. In March 1990 a woman walked into the Central Police Station in Newport having seen something unusual by the side of the road.

Linda Vines, a teacher from Cwmfelinfach, Caerphilly, reported seeing two bags in a lay-by as she drove along the A467 Rogerstone bypass on Wednesday, 21 March 1990.

She saw no vehicle parked there, but said, "I saw two bags, side by side, on the grass verge, one was red in colour and the other was dark." She thought someone had accidentally left their luggage in the lay-by and went to the police station to report it.

Jeff Harris was the officer on duty who was sent to investigate. "I was a stone's throw away from the lay-by," he recalled. "I pulled into that lay-by, got out of the police vehicle and started to examine the bags. Initially, I just felt around the bags to see if I could feel what was inside. There was one large bag and a smaller bag, a kit bag. As I felt the smaller one I thought, *It feels like portions of meat inside.*

"So, I went back to the big bag, felt that – that was quite sort of square and solid." He returned to the small bag and undid the zip. Inside were blue and white striped bags of the kind they used to have in supermarkets. He said, "I felt inside one and I could feel knuckles, like joints and bone joints. I thought, *Is this portions of meat in here?* So I ripped one bag, looked at it, and I could see sort of skin and hairs. *Is it pork?* And then a further look down, but the hairs were too fine for a pig and the skin was a lot darker.

"I ripped the bag again, and got the impression that perhaps I was looking at a forearm. Have I got a body here, this is the arms and leg in this bag? And is that the torso in the big bag?" He inspected the big bag again and suspected it contained a human torso. He got on his radio and told the dispatcher, "I don't want to cause alarm, but I think I got something suspicious here." He requested that a scenes of crime officer (SOCO) come along for a second opinion.

Constable Alyn Chown was the SOCO with Gwent Police who attended. "I put my gloves and suit on, walked across to where Jeff Harris was, and I could see that he was looking at possibly a forearm within one of the bags. I then opened the second bag, the larger of the two, like a rucksack. Inside, when I ripped the bag open, was the chest, including a nipple, of what appeared to be a male. I immediately closed the bag up and called for the assistance of colleagues and a Home Office pathologist."

Detective Chief Superintendent Mark Waters arrived with Dr Stephen Leadbetter, the Home Office pathologist.

He confirmed that it was a man's torso. The remains were taken to the Royal Infirmary in Cardiff, where Dr Leadbetter conducted the post-mortem.

Mark Waters was the head of CID in the Gwent force. "I had a call to attend the Rogerstone bypass, a rather strange call to say that a police officer there thinks he's got a body on the side of the road. It's one o'clock, I think, on an afternoon, it was a rather strange time, daylight, lots of people, traffic about. But sure enough, when I got to the lay-by there were two bags on the edge of the road, and a young police officer there said, 'I think there's a body in it.'"

The sight inside the rucksack, along with the smell, confirmed that. "I said, 'Yeah, you're right, son. This is a dead-un.' So, I then set everything in motion, called for the forensic team. I spoke to the pathologist, then started to organise ourselves, called for an incident room in Maindy, and the investigation was under way."

Chown related what happened at the post-mortem. "We had a forensic scientist attend the post-mortem, which is a little bit unusual, we don't normally do that. But because we found that all the limbs had been wrapped in black bags, we had an expert to come and assist us in removing the body parts from those bags. They were then looked at by the pathologist to determine the cause of death, and the bags were exhibited and given to the forensic science service to do their examination.

"We looked at the body parts. It looked as though the body had been washed, as there was little blood evident even within the black bags. Also, the body had been jointed – the body had been dismembered from the joints – which was a little bit unusual. This suggested that whoever had done it may well have had some anatomical knowledge. A doctor, surgeon, butcher, something along those lines."

Mark Waters awaited a call from Dr Leadbetter. When it came it was not what the detective wanted to hear. Waters said, "Needless to say, I was a bit disappointed when he said, 'Well, you've got a torso and arms, we've got legs, but we've got no hands and we've got no head.' So, I realised then that we were probably going to have a difficult case."

The incident room was equipped with a HOLMES computer (Home Office Large Major Enquiry System) and trained operators. This was introduced for UK police forces after the much-criticised Yorkshire Ripper inquiry and allowed police to collate and cross-check huge amounts of data gathered during major cases. This logged every decision taken by Waters and his team – every statement, car reported, phone call, and action. It was all set up at speed, which was just as well, because information started flowing into the investigation later that afternoon. This was spurred on by a press conference that Waters gave, appealing to the public for witnesses who may have been on the bypass.

A major problem was that there were no marks of violence on the body parts to indicate a cause of death, and with no head or hands, identification was almost impossible. The bags, therefore, became the focus of inquiries. The zips and catches on the rucksack were traced to a batch of bags sold in Australia and South-East Asia, but mainly New Zealand, which gave the police somewhere to start. Missing persons records were scoured, but nothing could be found for a man of this description – aged 20 to 35, gingery hair.

Waters was beginning to feel frustrated at the lack of a good lead in terms of identifying this victim or information on the car that dropped off the bags. One piece of good news came when another motorist stepped forward to contact the team. "We did get one man who said that he did see a person drop the bags off," Waters said, "and he said he had a good look at the person. We tried to do an identikit, but it wasn't very good. But he did say he could recognise the man again."

This man, Robert Clark, a 31-year-old florist, said he had been driving along the bypass shortly before 1 pm and saw a white or cream-coloured small car, something like a Metro or Fiesta. He saw a man on foot outside the car with a reddish brown holdall. The witness said this man was white, aged 35 to 50, "not stocky", about five foot six to five foot ten. "I would say that his hair was dark and receding at the front," the witness said.

On the following Sunday came the breakthrough that Det Ch Supt Waters and his team needed badly. Linda Watkins was an officer working in the major incident room in Newport. She recalled, "After a late lunch, I took a call from, I believe, a farmer in the coastal area of Newport Duffryn. This was some days after the torso had been discovered, and he reported to me that he had found what he believed to be a human head and hands in some plastic bags on his farmland.

He was quite alarmed. He knew about the murder because it had been on the media throughout the days previously. So, he obviously connected the two things and thought that what he had found was connected to the murder."

The farmer's statement makes for macabre reading. Derek David, aged 28, owned a 150-acre farm at St Brides, Fair Orchard Farm. Because it was lambing season, he had employed a farmhand, Andrew Newberry, who was in his early twenties. Newberry approached his boss out in a field and said, "There's a head in the bag over there." Hardly able to believe what Newberry had said, David went to have a look at a red kitbag lying in the field. Newberry insisted he could feel a nose and ear, but the contents were covered in some tape. David went to get a knife, while Newberry chased a sheep. When he returned, they inspected a Tesco bag in a ditch, which Newberry opened. "Oh, there's hands," he said.

Mark Waters explained what followed. "On the Sunday lunchtime, if I remember it was Mothering Sunday, I had a phone call to say they'd found the head and the hands. A farmer had reported finding these in a hedge near Wentlooge." This is a beautiful, but quiet, stretch of marshes between Cardiff and Newport, close to the coast. It is an ideal spot to dispose of a body, but the killer had chosen not to conceal the bags, so they were found quickly. Had the head and hands been hidden or disposed of more effectively, it could have been a major hindrance to identifying the victim. Yet the killer did not seem to care if they were found. This raised the question of whether the perpetrator cut the body up to make it easier to dispose of, or because dismemberment was something he enjoyed.

Waters' most immediate priority now was to build up a picture of who the victim was. "I said, whatever you do, find out what they were wrapped in," he recalled. "The bag that the head and hands were in was made by DuPont, and it had a serial number on it."

The first clue detectives discovered was that this kit bag was sold in Australia and New Zealand, but the bulk of them were in the latter country. The next step was to identify the head. An attempt to produce an identikit likeness of the victim's face was poor, and it was decided not to release the image to the public. Det Ch Insp William Glynn was tempted to release a photo of the face, but this was deemed too gruesome. Glynn had been among the officers who attended the initial discovery of body parts on the Rogerstone bypass. He had been made senior investigating officer under Det Ch Supt Waters and given a team of 40 officers. "I had been a policeman for quite a long time and dealt with many serious crimes," he said. "But this was definitely going to be the most serious one I dealt with."

WILLIAM GLYNN,
DETECTIVE, GWENT CID

An artist drew an impression of the victim's face and this was published in the *South Wales Argus*. The police received no useful feedback from that. However, staff at the paper informed the investigators that they had a graphics department, one of whom was a talented artist. Some new software was then used by this artist to reconstruct the face, which provided a more realistic representation of the man's appearance. The newspaper then ran this image in its next edition. This time the response was immediate and unequivocal.

David Tully, from Newport, who had visited his relatives in New Zealand back in the 1970s, came forward after the *Argus* published its picture. His cousin Clive had recently been paying a return visit to Newport to catch up with the Welsh side of the family. He had stayed at a pub, the Waterloo Hotel, run by David's sister in Newport, before getting the building job in Bristol. David explained what happened after the *Argus* picture came out: "Someone who was a frequent visitor to my sister's pub came in one night after the picture had been put in the local newspaper. He said he thought it looked a lot like Clive. My sister said, 'No, it can't be, he's over in Bristol.' She phoned me, I went to the Maindy police station and spoke with the officer there. He showed me some drawing and pictures of Clive's head. I identified him, and one thing led to another." The fact that Tully was a New Zealander clearly tied in with the bag containing the body parts likely being from the same country, possibly belonging to the victim.

The picture was published on a Thursday, and on the following day there was another, separate, identification of Clive. "On the Friday morning a chap walked in and said, 'Look, I saw the graphic image in the Argus yesterday,'" said Mark Waters. "He said, 'I think I know who that is, but I'm not sure.' And I said, 'Well, who do you think it is?' And he said, 'I think it's a chap called Tully. I worked with him for a company in Weston-super-Mare. At the time, we were both lodging at the Waterloo pub in Newport. I can't be certain, but it does look like him.' I asked if he knew where he was. And he said, 'I think he went back to New Zealand.'"

Waters asked if the witness could face looking at a photograph of the head. "And he said, 'Yes, I can do that.' So, I brought the photograph, showed him, and he said to me, 'I've just been paid. If that isn't Clive Tully I'll give you my wages.' I said, 'Why are you so sure?' He said, 'Because that's exactly how he looked when I used to wake him up in the morning – he was terrible at getting up. That's him. That is Clive Tully.'"

The witness told detectives that Tully had a building society account in Newport and used to draw money at a branch in Bridge Street. The police talked to the manager who, though restricted in what information he could give out about an account, did confirm that Tully had withdrawn his last £20 about three or four days previously. This placed Tully in Newport four days before the body was found.

Detectives were dispatched to Weston-super-Mare to interview the builder who had employed Clive Tully. This man, Michael Higgins, was found on a building site and told the officers he had seen Tully at some flats he owned in Bristol just the other day. He had rented one to Tully for a while. When he last saw Tully, he was in the adjoining flat of a man called Green. The builder had said to Tully that he had thought he was going to return to New Zealand, but clearly he had changed his plans.

The detectives took the builder to his property in Luxton Street, Bristol. Malcolm Green was not at home, but Higgins said he had the key to the flat. On entering it with the officers, the builder said the layout of the flat had been switched around – the living room and bedroom had been swapped. When blood was then found under a bed, it became apparent that the furniture shuffling had been done to cover it up. Some of Tully's belongings were also found, along with a parole letter of Green's, revealing that he had a conviction for murder in Cardiff. Tully's DNA and fingerprints would later also be found in the flat.

The Gwent officers had already liaised with their colleagues in Bristol for the Luxton Street visit. Mark Waters called Bristol CID and said, "Look, we're on your patch, we think we've got a murder. The murder took place on your patch. Will you send your scenes of crime to this house?"

Former detective chief inspector Glyn recalled: "There was blood leading up the stairs. And subsequently, blood was found in the pipes of the bath. All that blood was identified as having come from Clive Tully and not from Malcolm Green or anybody else." The patch of blood that had been covered with the bed was around 46 inches square. In addition, the carpet under it had been cut and scrubbed with detergent. Glynn discovered that Green had a girlfriend, Helen Barnes. When officers turned up at her family's home in Fishponds, Bristol, neighbours revealed they had all gone out for a meal. The detectives waited, and then when Green returned at 11.25pm on 30 March, a Detective Inspector Baynham said to Green, "I am arresting you on suspicion of the murder of Clive Tully."

His response was, "Clive Tully dead? He's my friend! I don't understand. Clive Tully dead? Me arrested? It's all a big mistake."

Det Ch Insp Glynn said, "I was the officer who did the majority of the interviewing. I was assisted by an officer from Bristol because the murder had taken place in Bristol.

"Malcolm Green was an extremely cool character. He was well educated, a very fit-looking individual. He obviously looked after himself. He was smart. And he was the sort of guy that I feel would definitely appeal to ladies, a very self-assured type of person. He was well able to answer every question that was put to him. He had a solicitor present, but surprisingly enough, he very, very infrequently referred to the solicitor before answering every single question. I found this unusual because most people we interview for serious crimes are usually no-commenting, or if they answer, they answer just the question you ask them. But Green seemed as if he wanted to tell us everything that he could and try to turn us away from the scene." Despite this, Glynn added, "It seemed as if he enjoyed being interviewed."

Perhaps Green really did enjoy the attention. He had been caught in 1971 because he could not resist taunting the police via several phone calls over the murder of Glenys Johnson. In 1990 he had taken unnecessary risks in disposing of Clive Tully. Clive's folks in Newport thought that Clive was return-ing home to New Zealand from Spain or Portugal. They even had a party for him, according to Mark Waters, and gave him money towards his air fare. However, he had returned to the

UK, probably because he was low on funds. Then, of course, he reconnected with Green and asked to stay with him.

Because his relatives in Wales and New Zealand had no idea where he was, his disappearance may not have been noticed for a long time. "Green would have known all of this, you know, that nobody's going to miss this guy," Waters said. But Green had blundered. Why he chose to drive from Bristol, around the Bristol Channel, across the Severn Bridge, and on to Newport to leave the body parts on the Rogerstone bypass is a mystery. Not only was this the one area where Clive Tully was known to locals and might be identified, but Green must have realised he could be witnessed dropping off the bags on the busy road.

Look at the body deposition sites at the Rogerstone bypass and Fair Orchard. The Waterloo Hotel owned by Clive's cousin is situated between these sites – they are all within walking distance of each other. Leaving Clive's body in bags so close to the hotel where he was known was clearly a provocative act by Green.

Constable Alyn Chown, the scenes of crime officer who attended the initial discovery of body parts, believes that Green's apparent blunders – openly leaving the bags by the road, depositing the head and hands where they could easily be discovered – were not blunders at all. He explained: "I honestly believe he wanted to be caught. There were lots of places that he could have hidden the body. He came over the Severn Bridge. He could have put them over the side into the river. He came past Chepstow. He could have gone up to the forest and hidden the body up there, never to be found again. He left the body where he did, as he did with his first murder, in order to taunt the police and perhaps even assist them in catching him. I don't believe he tried to disguise what he did at all. He wrapped the body in those black plastic bags, leaving his fingerprints on them, which eventually he was identified by. And never at any time did he give an explanation for his actions, either in interview or in court. I just genuinely believe he committed the murders with the chance that he knew that he was going to be caught."

Perhaps what Green wanted was the irreconcilable duality of evading the police while revelling in the notoriety and recognition of being a brutal murderer. While he probably did not want to be caught, perhaps at some subliminal level he took risks that could expose his brutal crime.

He claimed he had not been at the flat when the murder was committed. On the day the body was taken to the Newport area, Green said he was in Avonmouth looking for work. "Once we questioned him further about that, he was unable to provide any alibi of any person he'd spoken to regarding the job," Glynn said. "So, he tried to compensate for that by saying that when he got there, he decided the job wasn't for him, so he wasn't actually interviewed. He also said that he'd gone to a pub in the Bristol area. Subsequent inquiries revealed that nobody could remember him being in there at that time, although it was his local and they knew him."

For all his calm and self-assurance, Green seemed to think he could just lie and lie, and the police would be too gullible to check what he was saying. "He could have been more evasive," Glynn said. "He denied having his girlfriend's car [the Metro seen on the bypass by the witness], then he admitted to having it. The car was seen by three people at the scene where the bags had been dumped, and one person positively identified him. And that person said that he had a particularly good look at him because he thought he'd broken down and he was going to give him a hand."

The examination of Green's flat and checks on his criminal record revealed disturbing aspects to the man in custody. There was his interest in biology – he had been studying it at technical college – and a chart found in his house showed various joints in the human body. There was his past working in a slaughterhouse, and, of course, his horrendous murder and mutilation of Glenys Johnson almost 20 years before. "We questioned him about whether he'd ever dissected any human, any animals before. He said he hadn't, other than slugs. But I don't know whether that was true or not."

Green's fixation on body parts, mutilation and his known propensity for massive violence fitted with what police then knew of Tully's murder. Three decades later, retired detective chief inspector Glynn gave his own insight into what happened at the Luxton Street flat. "I personally feel that he didn't plan the crime. I think there was an argument, he wanted Tully to leave the flat. He'd put Tully up in the flat and he wanted Tully to leave because he felt that the owner of the flat wouldn't approve of Tully being there. And as a result of that, he might lose his own flat. So he wanted Tully to leave, and it appears to me that Tully was arguing against that. And as a result, an argument ensued, and Green killed him. There were at least 13 blows to his head. It was a particularly vicious attack. It wasn't an accidental death or just something where he was trying to get rid of him. It was obviously an attack with the intention of killing him." It was suspected that Green hit Tully with an implement such as a hammer.

The evidence that the police gathered against Green was extensive. There was Tully's DNA, fingerprints and blood at the flat. One of the bags containing body parts was found to have been given to Green on his release from prison. Green's fingerprints were found on the rucksack containing the torso. The motorist Robert Clark had given police a valuable account of having seen Green at the Rogerstone lay-by where Clive Tully's torso and limbs were discovered on 21 March. The white car he had seen, a Mini Metro, had belonged to Green's girlfriend. The witness also picked out Green in an identity parade. Furthermore, none of Green's would-be alibis could be corroborated.

Many other factors explained how Green had tried to cover up his crime, Glyn explained further. "He wouldn't let people into the flat after it had happened. He tried to disguise the odour of the deceased by buying flowers, by using a smelly aftershave and detergent. He wouldn't allow the windows to be shut in his girlfriend's car when there were a couple of her friends in it. Although they were cold, he wouldn't let that window be shut, which indicated to me that he was trying to hide the smell from the car."

When Green was charged with the murder of Tully, there were no histrionics, despite the suspect's volatile temper. Glynn said, "There was no reaction at all. He just seemed to accept it and shrug. There didn't seem to be a great deal of reaction from him about anything, to be honest."

Green told his interviewers he was probably Clive Tully's best friend in the UK. He told them he had put Tully up in his flat after he returned from Spain and Portugal, and lent him money. "He spent Christmas with me and my girlfriend because he had nowhere else to go," Green said. "He was lonely while he was over here. In fact, I took him down to see my parents in Cardiff." Green said he had not seen the New Zealander since the day he had agreed to let him stay in Luxton Street.

The trial at Bristol Crown Court began on 23 October 1990. It lasted seven days. Glynn's boss, Det Ch Supt Waters, never interviewed Green, but he did watch him during the trial. "I sat behind him, at the back of the court. I watched his movements, he just looked straight ahead, no expression on his face. A very cold man, really just cold. He was a shortish man, bald head. Nothing about him really, but quite serious, well-spoken, and I would say he was quite an intelligent man."

Waters revealed that there was often a wager riding on the timing of the verdict. "We used to have a bet on how long the jury would take to come back," he said. "Prosecution counsel, defence counsel, solicitors, police. It was like a sweep, and we put a time when we thought the jury would come back, and the person who came closest had the kitty. And I put half past eleven because it was such a short, such an obvious case, and Green didn't even give evidence in his defence. Well, quarter past eleven went past, quarter past twelve went past, quarter past one went past – it was now lunch time."

The detective rang the Home Office at 2.30 pm to ask if he would have to release Green from custody if he was acquitted, because Green was still on parole. A reply came back that did not please the chief superintendent: yes, he must be released if acquitted.

"Half past three came by, it came to four o'clock, quarter past four, and the judge called the jury back for a majority verdict," Waters said. "They walked back in and they were sort of talking amongst themselves as they got to the jury box. And then suddenly the foreman said, 'We've got a unanimous verdict.' And the verdict was guilty."

Green shouted at the jury, "You are wrong," finally giving the court a glimpse of the rage behind the calm exterior. The killer's veneer of respectability could be seen for the sham it was.

He also threw his arms open wide and said to his girlfriend, "I didn't do it." To which she replied, "I'll wait for you."

The jury had not been told of Green's previous murder conviction, because at this time the accused's past record was inadmissible. However, once he had been found guilty, the police then addressed the court to announce his 1970 murder of Glenys Johnson. "And suddenly this young lady in the jury started becoming hysterical with crying," Waters said, "and she'd obviously be holding the jury up all day. For what reason I do not know, but that's juries for you. But he was convicted."

He was sentenced once again to life, to serve at least 25 years. However, Home Secretary Kenneth Baker later changed the tariff to a whole-life sentence. This time, Malcolm Green would die in prison.

Speaking at the time of the sentencing, Det Ch Supt Waters expressed his anger that Green had ever been released after his conviction for the terrible murder of Glenys Johnson. "He's a dangerous man who should never have been let loose on the public again. He cold-bloodedly cut up a man who was supposed to be his friend.

"I would like to know who was responsible for letting him go and on what grounds, and I believe they should answer for it. You can never be sure a killer won't strike again."

After sentencing, Det Ch Insp Glynn described Green as a "psychopath". He even said psychiatric reports had recommended Green was not fit to be released from prison. His quote at the time was: "Of all the people I have interviewed, Green is probably the most dangerous and probably the most calculating. He is the most cold-blooded, calculating killer, who shows no remorse for his actions. He thought he was able to beat the police."

Today, the case still stands out for the former senior investigating officer. "He was very clever in a lot of things he did," Glynn said. "But having gone to all that trouble of cutting a body up like that, I still find it extremely strange – and this really sticks in my mind – why he didn't just get rid of those parts by burying them in various places. He, in fact, took them back to the one place where Clive Tully would have been known, which was the Newport area. He could have taken them anywhere, and we would have probably never found who the deceased was, because nobody had reported Clive missing."

That Green had returned to murder just five months after being released on parole still shocked Glynn as well. "It's very disturbing. It is unusual. There are a number of people that do get released from prison and commit a murder later on, but for it to be as quick as this is very unusual, I would suggest.

"He was extremely dangerous, very volatile. And I think that if he hadn't killed Clive Tully, it wouldn't have been long before he killed somebody else."

Clive Tully was a quiet young man who had come to the UK to connect with distant relatives. While staying at his cousin's Waterloo Hotel, he had got to meet family members, such as his cousin Norman Tully. Norman had been able to show Clive a photo of his father, Joseph, whom he had never known or even seen (Joseph died when Clive was three). The cousin arranged for prints to be made of Joseph, which he could give Clive. He said, "I would describe Clive as being quiet, but happy and pleased that he had met some of the family."

Clive's mother, Betty Goodwin, would later tell police from New Zealand, "It was always his dream to visit his relatives in Wales, his father's family." He had done every job he could – tree planting, car washing, labouring – to save the money for his UK visit.

Sadly, Clive had the terrible misfortune to befriend Malcolm Green while in Bristol. To further compound the tragedy of his adventure, it seems his trip was partly motivated by the death of his grandmother in New Zealand. Therein lies further heartbreak.

Mark Waters found out more about Clive's background during the police investigation. He recalled, "Tully's father was born and bred in Newport. He was a merchant seaman, and he was married. He jumped ship in New Zealand. He married Tully's mother bigamously. He then died from a heart attack.

"Tully's mother remarried, had another family. Clive Tully then went to live with his grandmother, that's his mother's mother. She was tragically killed. When gran died, he didn't really have anybody. And that's when he decided to come over to trace his father's relatives. He came to Newport. He met his cousins. One of his relatives was the landlady of the Waterloo pub, and then he worked for this chap in Weston-super-Mare. He was staying at the Waterloo and working at Weston-super-Mare. And then he went to live in Bristol. He rented a flat off his employer that was next door to Green."

David Tully, Clive's cousin in Newport, revealed what actually happened to Clive's grandmother, which added what must have been an almost unbearable further layer of emotional pain for the family. David said, "Some years previously in New Zealand, someone who was in prison for rape, I believe it was, warned the powers that be over there that if ever he was let out, he would probably kill, and it wouldn't be safe on the streets. As it happened, he was allowed out. Clive's grandmother was then raped and killed. She was in her eighties at the time, which must've been devastating for the whole family. So, to then lose Clive on top of that? Absolutely horrendous. It hit the family in many, many different ways, and it's still affected them to this day, from what I can understand."

DAVID TULLY,
CLIVE TULLY'S COUSIN

The sheer appalling coincidence of having two family members murdered by men who had been released from prison in error must have been incredibly painful to live with all these years.

Like Det Ch Supt Waters, David Tully condemned the decision to release Green from prison. "I can't understand how the parole board in this country allowed him to walk free having committed one murder, and the judge in that trial said this man is too dangerous to be allowed out on the street again. The parole board decided this man was safe to be let out on the street. Unfortunately, those who sit on the parole board don't have to answer to anyone if they make a mistake. They can just move on to the next case. Sadly, for people like Clive, they pay the consequences of their mistakes."

David attended every day of Green's trial. He felt, as the only member of the family who had gone out to New Zealand to meet Clive's nearest and dearest, that he should be there.

All these decades later, David still feels the loss, that Clive missed the happy life he should have had. "I knew Clive initially as a small child running up the driveway to his mother's home when I went to New Zealand the first time. Then to have his life ended in a flat somewhere in Bristol… I feel it's sad, it's a sad end. His family will have lost a great deal. He should now be in the prime of his life. He should be married, he should have children and he should be living a happy, wonderful life, but sadly that was all taken away from him.

"Clive had the world in front of him, and all that was taken away."

LOUISA MAY MERRIFIELD

Blackpool

10

"As wicked and cruel a murder as I ever heard tell of"

Blackpool, 1953
Victim: Sarah Ann Ricketts
Murderer: Louisa May Merrifield

The past may be a foreign country, but in 1953 Blackpool was more like a disturbing hall of mirrors on the Pleasure Beach. Few people were what they appeared to be.

On 10 March 1953 the *West Lancashire Evening Gazette* carried a classified advert. It read: "Resp. woman or couple share furn. house rent-free for service to lady. 339 Devonshire Rd, Blackpool."

The lady was Sarah Ann Ricketts. She was 79 years old and housebound, in that she could not venture further than her garden. She lived in a two-bedroomed bungalow on a pleasant road that ran partly alongside the North Shore Golf Club and parallel to the Blackpool sea front.

The attraction of living rent-free in return for looking after the old woman drew several applicants. Two days later, on Thursday 12 March, the successful "respectable" couple, Louisa and Alfred Merrifield, moved in and took up their housekeeping duties.

This arrangement is quite revealing about the way people lived in the years after the Second World War. Clearly, looking after an elderly woman and living rent-free – no pay was mentioned – was a good deal for quite a few people. Money was scarce for many working people, who moved frequently from rented rooms to rented rooms in search of something affordable and decent. Louisa and Alfred had themselves been fairly itinerant, on occasion leaving their boarding house without actually paying the rent.

As for Sarah Ricketts, who was a widow, it may seem strange to us that such a vulnerable old woman would welcome two complete strangers to care for her on the basis of one interview. It was not as if home helps did not exist at this time. Mrs Ricketts herself had had one for a couple years, who left only a month before the Merrifields were employed. Her name was Lavinia Blezard, and she was provided by the Blackpool Corporation, the local authority. She had done all Mrs Ricketts' cooking, cleaning, mending, washing and ironing, as well as drawing her pension of £1.12.6d (one pound, twelve shillings and sixpence) from the local post office. Why her role with the pensioner had ended is not clear. Perhaps it was because she only attended Mrs Ricketts three days a week and the pensioner needed full-time care. Or perhaps it was because Mrs Ricketts was not easy to please. "She was cute, wayward, wilful and very selfish," Lavinia Blezard said.

Mrs Ricketts was certainly wilful enough to employ the Merrifields after one look at them. And so this rather odd married couple became her full-time companions and carers.

Louisa was 46 years old and had been married to Alfred for two and a half years. One woman who encountered her said she was a little over five feet tall, "well built, tight-lipped". In some photos she looks as formidable as Ena Sharples, the fictional sour-faced gossip of TV soap *Coronation Street*. At the age of 71, husband Alfred was 25 years older than Louisa. What had been the attraction? Not the ecstasy of love, apparently. "This old bugger [her husband] told me he had money," Louisa said, "but when I married him I found he had nowt."

They both had backgrounds that mixed hardship and lawbreaking. Crime historian Dr Nell Darby said of Louisa, "She was from a humble background. She was born in Wigan. Her father was actually from West Bromwich and worked in the mines. So, he'd moved north in search of work. Her family was a large one, and there would have been a lot of mouths to feed on a limited income. And the children would have needed to work as soon as they were old enough. The 1911 Census is quite sad. It shows Louisa as the youngest child, then aged five, and that her parents had 12 children, and by 1911 five of them had already died. So, this was quite a difficult upbringing for her. It was poor. She would have seen siblings die, and you can understand why she was kind of drawn to Blackpool and to the opportunities it might have had, and also why money might have been important to her because it offered an escape from her background."

Louisa was born on 3 December 1906 in Wigan. She had an elementary education, was an average student and left school at the age of 13, which was common for working-class children at the time. Louisa then went to work in a cotton mill, where she remained for six years. This was followed by another job that could be a grind: domestic service. Her next role was as a mother. She married Joseph Ellison in 1931 and had nine children, only four of whom survived into the 1950s. Ellison died in 1949. On 5 January 1950, Louisa wed again, this time to a Richard Weston. Extraordinarily, she was aged 43 at the time, while Weston was 80 years old. This union was ill-starred, and after just eight weeks Louisa's second husband also died – the cause of death, she said, being a heart attack. By the summer, she had married septuagenarian Alfred Merrifield at Wigan register office.

Questions about her unconventional marriages would resurface as events unfolded in the coming weeks.

Alfred's life had also been marked by hard work and premature death. He was born in Callington, Cornwall, on 24 August 1882, and came from a family of six children. His mother died when he was about eight years old, and he left school at the age of 12, beginning an apprenticeship with an engineering firm. He married Alice Whittle in 1902 and fathered 10 children. In 1915 he volunteered for the army to fight in the First World War, serving with the 200th Field Company, Royal Engineers, in France and Belgium. After demobilisation he had various spells of employment – as a labourer, foreman, moulder – and unemployment. In 1937, while working as a moulder for an engineering firm, he injured both of his legs. He needed treatment for six months, received £300 in compensation (about £21,000 in 2022), and never worked again. His wife died in Manchester in 1948.

By the time he and Louisa arrived on Sarah Ricketts' doorstep, they were making do on his weekly pension of £2.14.0d (two pounds, fourteen shillings) and a further £2 he received from the National Assistance Board, possibly for the disability caused by his job (totalling around £150 in 2022). Louisa had taken a variety of jobs, often in some domestic or housekeeping role. As a result of their precarious income, they were always on the lookout for cheap places to live.

Louisa and Alfred both had black marks against their characters, which they no doubt did not mention during their job interview with Sarah Ricketts. In the previous three years, Louisa had had around 20 jobs, suggesting she was not the most dependable employee to have working in your home. In 1946 she had been found guilty of ration-book fraud, apparently having used ration books that were not hers to get extra food or clothes. She was sentenced to 84 days' imprisonment because she refused to pay the £10 fine. While she was locked up, her children were taken into care. "It's possible that she was committing minor offences before that time, and this is just the one that she got caught for," Dr Darby said.

In 1949, Alfred appeared at Wigan Magistrates' Court charged with indecently assaulting an eight-year-old girl. He was fined £25 (about £950 in 2022).

According to Alfred, their move from Wigan to Blackpool began in April 1951, when Louisa got work as a cook with the Blackpool Tower Company. Wigan is only 30 miles from

Blackpool and the huge seaside resort, with its Golden Mile beachfront, theatres, bed and breakfasts, and hotels, would have probably offered more job opportunities than Louisa's home town. "Blackpool, then and now, and arguably back into Victorian times, had been a Mecca for working-class people to go and have a break, to experience a bit of glamour," said Dr Darby. "Bright lights, lots of entertainment. In this period, foreign holidays weren't as common as they are now."

Alfred followed Louisa to the resort, and for the next year or so they led a nomadic life moving between rental rooms as Louisa took on "several different domestic situations", as her husband put it. If their relationship had ever enjoyed a honeymoon period, it was ancient history by now. The landlady of one of their boarding houses, Margaret Gardner, described the goings-on: "The Merrifields quarrelled frequently in my house, calling each other names and swearing at each other. He used to hit her with a stick after she struck him. During one of these quarrels I was present in the dining room of my house. Apparently, Mrs Merrifield had taken Mr Merrifield's pension book and got his money stopped. Amongst the things I heard Mr Merrifield say to her was that she was trying to do him in."

It is likely this combustible, rather shifty couple quickly realised there was potentially more on offer at 339 Devonshire Road than free accommodation. To her new live-in carers, Sarah Ricketts was wealthy and secure. She owned and lived in a lovely bungalow, worth up to £4,000 (around £118,000 today), in a desirable area of Blackpool. And she had money.

Mrs Ricketts had been married twice. Her second husband, William John Ricketts, a retired farmer, had died in 1946 and left her rental income from a house he owned and interest from investments. His estate was valued at £4,493 (around £130,000 today). Certainly, to Louisa, her new employer – like many before her – had a life the housekeeper could only dream of. For women with Louisa's impoverished background, there were virtually only three options in life: the mill, domestic service, or marriage. And like many working-class women at this time, she had probably married not for love, but for security, and to escape from her over-populated, struggling family. However, after marrying three times, she still was tramping between dismal lodgings and dead-end

DR NELL DARBY

jobs, leaving the latter because of her poor attitude, laziness or suspected thieving. She would later tell police they had moved addresses in Blackpool around 20 times.

Dr Nell Darby suspected that Louisa had grown more cynical and opportunistic as she got older. "You do wonder what her motivations were," she said. "Was she going into jobs to see what she could steal, what she could get out of this job? I suspect Louisa changed over time. Originally, she would have got a job because she actually intended to work, and maybe saw opportunities to steal or to commit other crimes. As time goes on, she realises that this is a good way of getting into a household, of being able to commit crime. So, then she has more of a criminal mentality when she takes on a job. I think there's probably a development over time and a change in the way she looks at jobs and what she can get out of them."

She and Alfred were no doubt on their best behaviour when they arrived at Devonshire Road. Sarah Ricketts was four feet eight inches tall, but she was not to be pushed around. The home help's description of her as "wayward, wilful and very selfish" would have been seconded by her daughters. Loveday Whitaker, aged 56, was married and lived in Stoke-on-Trent. She would say she had not fallen out with her mother, but admitted she rarely saw her and did not know the Merrifields were looking after her. Ethel Harrison, 57, lived a 20-minute walk away from her mother on Collins Avenue, but may as well have been in Stoke with her sister, so rarely did she visit Mrs Ricketts. "She was a very difficult person to deal with, so we decided to let her have her own way and live her own life," Mrs Harrison said. Her mother had had a number of different people living in the bungalow, between her marriages and since the death of her second husband, and all had left after falling out with her.

Stubborn and selfish as she might be, by this time Sarah Ricketts had got to the stage where she was badly in need of care and assistance. She had had a fall around 18 months previously and never now ventured beyond the garden gate. A concerned neighbour might get the fire going for her or make a meal, but by and large she was on her own. The coal man, grocer and milkman making deliveries would all let themselves into the bungalow because she could no longer answer the door.

Louisa found the old lady was unwell when she arrived and persuaded her to go to bed. There was no food in the house, but Louisa did find bottles of Guinness and spirits, which Mrs Ricketts said she took for her asthma. Louisa put this right by buying food and giving Mrs Ricketts proper meals, "fish and chicken and a good pudding every day", as Louisa said. Mrs Ricketts' health improved.

The pensioner certainly appreciated the help she was receiving. According to Alfred, she told Louisa, "If you do justice to me and look after me, I will see that you have got a home for life." Mrs Ricketts then, again according to Alfred, told Louisa to send for her solicitor.

On 24 March, just 12 days after moving in, Louisa was at the offices of solicitor William Darbyshire. She informed him that on behalf of Mrs Ricketts he was to draw up a new will for his client in which she, Louisa Merrifield, would be sole executrix and beneficiary.

Darbyshire arrived at the bungalow on 31 March with his clerk, Clara Marchant. At some point, Alfred buttonholed the solicitor and told him that he was to be included in the will as joint beneficiary with his wife. It would appear that husband and wife were jockeying independently of each other to get into that will. They, however, were asked to leave the room while Darbyshire questioned Sarah Ricketts. He asked why she wanted to change her will. She replied that her two daughters had never been good to her, and that Mr and Mrs

Merrifield had promised to look after her. She wanted to leave everything to them, she said, confirming that Alfred should be included as beneficiary. Darbyshire and his clerk witnessed her signing the new will.

Exactly two weeks later, Sarah Ricketts was dead.

The events of those two weeks would be closely examined at the trial later that year.

If the Merrifields had made a good initial impression on Mrs Ricketts, this did not last. Having helped to revive Mrs Ricketts with fulsome meals, Louisa and her employer then had a falling out. Mrs Ricketts had initially given Louisa control of her budget so that she could order food. One provision the bungalow was not short of was alcohol, with deliveries of rum and Guinness arriving regularly, and one order of a bottle of champagne and a case of Mackeson's thrown in after the Merrifields arrived. However, when, during the third week of the Merrifield's employment, Mrs Ricketts tried to order two bottles of rum and a bottle of brandy, along with butter and sugar, Louisa told her there was not enough money for these items. Mrs Ricketts' response was that she could afford them before Louisa and her husband had arrived. The outcome was that Mrs Ricketts took back control of the housekeeping budget, and the shopping emphasis switched back from food to booze again.

This and several other incidents indicate that Sarah Ricketts may have suspected that money was going missing. When the booze delivery man called on 13 April, she looked in her bag and found she had no money, nor could she find any in her drawer. Alfred was there and said he would go to the bank for her to see what she had in her account. The delivery man, Jerzy Forjan, said Mrs Ricketts replied, "When you go to the bank, call my solicitor to the house, because I want to change my will." Alfred then changed his mind and said it would be too far for him to go. She then turned to the delivery man and said, "He's all right, it's her [Louisa] I don't like. I am going to turn them out because she called me a bloody fool."

Jerzy Forjan's account is interesting in several respects. He was at the bungalow on the morning of the day before Mrs Ricketts died. She made clear she wanted to change her will, and Alfred seemed to refuse, or delay, summoning the solicitor when she asked him to. Did Mrs Rickett's intention to change the will again prompt the Merrifields – either together or singly – to kill her?

While the pensioner was vulnerable and perhaps suggestible (she agreed to hand the Merrifields her home after knowing them for only a fortnight), she could also be wilful, if not stroppy. On 9 April Mrs Ricketts looked unwell and Louisa asked who her doctor was. Mrs Ricketts replied that she had not seen a doctor for two years. When Louisa suggested a local man, Dr Albert Wood, Mrs Ricketts said she did not like him or his partners. Louisa proposed Dr Burton Yule instead. Mrs Ricketts replied, "I don't want that man near my door." Unknown to Mrs Ricketts, Louisa called on him anyway.

Dr Yule had had dealings with Mrs Ricketts before and did not want to do so again. Louisa insisted that he would be paid if he visited. He ended up agreeing to do so the next day, 10 April. Mrs Ricketts was not pleased and told him she did not want to see him when he arrived. Louisa was insistent that Mrs Ricketts needed examining – suggesting the pensioner might have a stroke that night – but she did not get her way and the patient refused to be examined. Instead, Dr Yule merely asked how Mrs Ricketts was getting on, and whether she had made her will. She said, "I am looking after them that look after me." He did not examine her, but apparently said, "You are quite *compos mentis* and know what you are doing."

It would appear that Louisa's real purpose in calling in Dr Yule to see "sick" Mrs Ricketts was to get him to issue a certificate stating that the old woman was, as he had said, in full control of her mental faculties and fit to sign her will. Dr Yule found this a peculiar request because the will had already been executed. When Louisa visited his surgery three days later, just the day before Mrs Ricketts' death, in order to pay the medical bill of 10 shillings and sixpence, Dr Yule refused to issue any certificate of mental well-being and said he wanted no involvement with a will. Instead of obtaining what she had clearly wanted – medical confirmation that Mrs Ricketts was mentally fit – what she got instead was Dr Yule able to see that the pensioner had been in good health when he saw her four days before her death. Indeed, he would tell police that the old lady had walked him to the garden gate, where she had told him that she did not trust the Merrifields, that they owed her money, and that she planned to change her will again.

After Dr Yule's visit, Sarah Ricketts went from being healthy for her age, as several witnesses would confirm, and having had no need of a doctor for two years, to suddenly falling seriously ill. The crucial period would be between when Dr Yule saw her on Friday 10 April, when she told him she was in good health and appeared active, to her death on Tuesday 14 April.

We only have Louisa and Alfred's version of the old woman's decline. Louisa said Mrs Ricketts was ill the evening after Dr Yule's visit. That night the old woman indulged in her favourite treat, jam, which she seemed to prefer to proper meals. She consumed a one-pound jar of Hartley's blackcurrant jam mixed with various spirits that evening. She was poorly the next day, Saturday. She had been "worried about her bowels". The next day her entire diet was five eggs, two of them beaten in brandy.

By Monday she was complaining of stomach pains. She ate two eggs in brandy and had a Guinness. This was the day Louisa visited Dr Yule to pay the bill. When she told him Mrs Ricketts was suffering, Dr Yule said he did not wish to attend to her, and Louisa should get Dr Albert Wood. Dr Wood saw Mrs Ricketts that evening. He said she looked better than when he had last seen her three years before. He diagnosed mild bronchitis, gave her a sedative, and prescribed a bottle of medicine for the next day. Despite the doctor saying Mrs Ricketts had nothing to worry about, Louisa said she was worried the old woman might die in the night. Again, despite a doctor concluding Mrs Ricketts had nothing to worry about, Louisa was raising the possibility of her imminent death. Before Dr Wood departed, the Merrifields were asked to leave the room. Once they had, Mrs Ricketts told him that the couple were trying to get rid of her and she was worried. He tried to reassure her and left. That night she drank brandy and rum. During the night Louisa said she found Mrs Ricketts sitting on the toilet rubbing her tummy.

LOUISA MERRIFIELD AND HUSBAND ALFRED
ON THEIR WAY TO POLICE HEADQUARTERS

She drank some more brandy and said, according to Louisa, "You don't know how ill I am."

On the Tuesday, Louisa went to Dr Wood's surgery and asked for someone to attend to Mrs Ricketts. A Dr Ernest Page came, found the pensioner unable to speak, and told Louisa he could not take her as his patient and she should refer the case back to Dr Yule. Louisa called three times at Dr Yule's surgery, but he was out. When he finally arrived at Devonshire Road at around 1.50 pm, he found Sarah Ricketts was dead.

Dr Yule was suspicious about her sudden demise. He would have well remembered Louisa's unusual request for certification of Mrs Ricketts' mental well-being. Professor Mike Berry, clinical forensic psychologist, pinpoints how Louisa's eagerness to protest her claim to the will backfired on her. "Mrs Ricketts was actually a healthy lady," Prof Berry said. "The GP says, 'Well, why did she die? She didn't have cancer. There was no terminal illness. She was elderly and she was not in great health, but she wasn't going to die within days.' And he therefore challenged right from the beginning that she died of natural causes, and therefore had the post-mortem done. Normally, if somebody dies and they're under the GP and in poor health, you wouldn't need a post-mortem. But Louisa had had a GP [Dr Yule] visit and the GP was convinced that she wasn't going to die immediately. That was the mistake."

Dr Yule refused to issue a death certificate. Instead, at around 2.30 pm, he phoned the police and spoke to Detective Sergeant Norman Steadman. Dr Yule suggested the sergeant also speak to Dr Wood. With both men deciding Mrs Ricketts was in no danger when they saw her, along with Louisa's fussing about the will and the old woman's comments to Dr Wood about fearing the Merrifields were trying to get rid of her, the police had sufficient grounds to investigate further.

Det Sgt Steadman, accompanied by a detective constable, went to 339 Devonshire Road and questioned the Merrifields. When asked if Mrs Ricketts had taken anything and what she had eaten, Louisa replied, "I think she had a stroke. She had eaten nothing all day, and nothing to drink except a few spots of rum and brandy." Louisa also said there was nothing in the house the dead woman could have taken that might have killed her.

Steadman detected no signs of injury or violence on Mrs Ricketts. He searched the house. In the kitchen he found no jam or empty jam jars. Mrs Ricketts' body was taken to Talbot Road Mortuary.

Superintendent Colin MacDougall went to the bungalow on 17 April. "We have strong reason to believe that Mrs Ricketts died as a result of something she had to eat or drink," he told Louisa.

"That's funny," she replied, "there has been nothing in this house since I've been here that would hurt her."

"As you know," the superintendent said, "we have searched the house and taken possession of certain articles but have not found any substance or container which would appear to account for her death."

Louisa became quite theatrical: "If my Maker sends for me now, my conscience is clear. There has never been anything in the house to hurt her."

Alfred's reaction to the superintendent's claim Mrs Ricketts died from something she had eaten was the same: "That can't be, she's had nothing to hurt her."

Louisa then told Supt MacDougall she had thrown out the jam jars containing Mrs Ricketts' favourite treat. Police suspected that whatever killed Mrs Ricketts was in the jam she ate so prodigiously.

Police made several searches of the bungalow. At this time, Mrs Ricketts' daughters had asked Det Sgt Steadman whether a diamond ring and gold wristwatch had been found. When, on 20 April, he returned to the bungalow and asked the Merrifields about these items, Louisa said, "Those are mine. Mrs Ricketts gave them to me on the day she died."

Unbeknown to the Merrifields, the evidence was growing that Sarah Ricketts' death had not been natural. At the post-mortem conducted by Dr George Bernard Manning on the night her death was discovered, he found that "the liver was extremely pale and showed toxic changes". The North-Western Forensic Science Laboratory ran tests and issued its report on 28 April, after which Dr Manning said he thought Mrs Ricketts had died from phosphorus poisoning. The stomach contents had also revealed evidence of bran, a compound found in Rodine rat poison.

For her part, Louisa portrayed herself as committed to looking after her employer, though she obviously saw nothing wrong in admitting she had stopped feeding her properly. "After about the third week here I would not accept the responsibility of providing the food for Mrs Ricketts, because she was spending too much on drink. I still did the household work and washed and dressed her, and sat up with her."

This worthiness in looking after Mrs Ricketts was the reason the Merrifields had been favoured in her will. Louisa claimed her wealth could not be left to her daughters because Mrs Ricketts said one of them was a thief who had stolen a fur from her, while the other, Ethel, was "one of the biggest prostitutes in Blackpool". Police would conclude that both women were "thoroughly respectable".

Calling in Dr Yule had had nothing to do with Mrs Ricketts' will, Louisa said, a claim that was also clearly not true.

Police discovered that just two days after the death, Louisa had gone to the funeral director on Church Street, George Johnson. She had told him that Mrs Ricketts did not want her daughters to know of the funeral arrangements and that she should be cremated. Johnson said only the next of kin could make such arrangements and sent her away. Did Louisa not realise her haste in wanting the body cremated – thereby destroying any proof of poisoning – and kept secret from the family would look suspicious? She clearly had no idea that the police would not accept her claims without rigorously investigating them, or that they had already tested the body for toxins.

The two doctors, Yule and Wood, had thought Mrs Ricketts looked relatively well in the days before her death. The grocery delivery man also saw her twice, including the day before she died, and said she seemed well. The van driver who brought the alcohol delivery spoke to her on the same day and said she seemed fine, while a neighbour confirmed she was up and about because he saw her in the garden on the afternoon before she died. If Sarah Ricketts was poisoned, it would appear a fatal dose was administered on the night of Monday 13 April, after all these witnesses saw her.

Detectives soon noticed further suspicious behaviour by Louisa – namely, that she could not help bragging about her impending inheritance.

Among those she boasted to was an acquaintance, Jessie Brewer. "We're all right. We're landed now. We went to live with an old girl and she died and left us a bungalow worth £4,000." The only problem was that this conversation occurred on Saturday 11 April – three days before Mrs Ricketts died. This, taken in conjunction with Louisa's other comments – that Mrs Ricketts had been "dying since we got here", "what if she dies in the night", "she might have a stroke at any moment" – strongly suggest the housekeeper was certain her employer was going to die, or was at least attempting to prime everyone to expect her death.

Police even heard of an extraordinary afternoon encounter Louisa had with a woman called Elizabeth Barraclough at a bus stop the day before the death. Louisa told this stranger that when she returned from a trip to Wigan she found her husband, Alfred, in bed with the old lady they were caring for. Louisa said they were "messing about". "I'll poison the old bugger and him as well," Louisa had reportedly told Mrs

Barraclough. She added that Louisa had said her husband had been trying to talk their employer into making him sole beneficiary of the will, though this was probably just Louisa voicing her suspicions.

There was a considerable amount of circumstantial evidence building against the Merrifields now, particularly against Louisa. Apart from the delivery man and one visitor – an acquaintance, Arthur Mather – they were the old woman's sole companions during the four weeks of their employment. Louisa's frequent referrals to Mrs Ricketts being close to death, particularly her remarks to Jessie Brewer, ran counter to the testimony of several witnesses, including two doctors, who thought the pensioner was looking well for her age. Louisa told Mrs Brewer and at least one other witness that she had been left a "lovely little bungalow" while Mrs Ricketts was still alive. Mrs Ricketts' comments to Dr Wood that the Merrifields were trying to get rid of her was disturbing in the light of her subsequent death. In addition, she had also told the delivery man she was "going to turn out" the couple after Louisa called her a bloody fool, and she said to Dr Yule she was going to change her will because she did not trust Alfred and Louisa.

Finally, the biggest doubt raised against the Merrifields, of course, was the apparent presence of rat poison in her body, when none could be found in the bungalow and Sarah Ricketts was not able to get to the shops. The clear possibility was that she had been deliberately fed the poison, probably disguised in her favourite jam, and the jam pots and poison had then been disposed of.

Further damning facts about Louisa came to light. Detectives found that she had bragged to Gertrude Thomas, a cook at their previous lodgings on Lytham Road, that she had "done in" two husbands already. "My last husband was 80, so it didn't take much to polish him off," was how Gertrude Thomas recalled their chat. "He fell through the bed and had a heart attack." The implication was that Louisa had fixed the bed so her second husband, Richard Weston, would fall. It was to Gertrude that Louisa said Alfred had lied about having his own money, when he actually had "nowt" – suggesting he was not worth killing.

Gertrude also revealed to police that the Merrifields had been ordered out of their rooms at Lytham Road, and she recalled the scene on their last day there. They were shouting at each other on the stairs, with Alfred saying to Gertrude, "See, missus, she carries rat poison in her bag." On an earlier occasion he had told Gertrude, "She's tried to do me in like she's done the others in, but she has found her mistake." That his wife was trying to poison him was a claim he repeated to several people. Other witnesses said they heard Louisa threatening to poison him.

Another visitor to Lytham Road, Alfred Dale, said that when Louisa was getting cigarettes out of her bag, he had seen in it a red box he recognised instantly as Rodine rat poison. He remembered it because at the time he thought it odd that she would be carrying poison around.

Poison had always been a discreet murder method and one that presented investigators with a host of problems.

Toxicologist Professor Robert Flanagan said, "Poisoning traditionally has been a difficult mechanism of murder to detect, because there's usually a separation between the assailant and the victim. If someone is stabbed or shot, there's a locus of where both people are together. Poisoning can be something which had been left in food or in drink, or given long-term to have an accumulative effect.

"In many countries now, this is the basis of legislation to stop dangerous compounds being available to potential murderers. Starting with the Arsenic Act from 1851, which was to try to keep track of very toxic compounds and have a register of people who possessed it – to limit access and thus use of the compound for homicidal purposes. Nowadays, many murders by poisoning are actually by people who, through their jobs or other contacts, have access to particular poisons. A classic case, of course, is Dr Harold Shipman, who had access to pharmaceutical diomorphine through his job as a general practitioner, and was able to administer it to patients without them really suspecting what he was doing."

The problem with Rodine in 1953 was that, while it could only be bought in a chemist's, for this poison, buyers did not have to sign a register.

Police put a huge effort into proving when and where Louisa or the couple together had bought the rat poison. They made inquiries at chemists' throughout Lancashire and held an identity parade at police HQ in Blackpool, but Louisa was not picked out.

What they were able to prove was that she had been using Mrs Ricketts' money to buy clothes for herself. She had used two of her employer's credit vouchers amounting to £40 (about £1,100 today) at various shops around Blackpool.

Becoming Mrs Ricketts' live-in carers had proved a huge change in fortune for the Merrifields. Police traced the many lodgings they had rented in Blackpool, where they heard many stories of the couple's arguments and accusations of poisoning plans. They also found that Louisa had done very little consistent work before arriving at Devonshire Road, and that the couple had been so hard up that Alfred had spent time in a hostel for the homeless.

Despite Louisa not being selected during the identification parade, police decided they had enough evidence of the couple's guilt. Following the identity parade on the afternoon of 30 April, a Detective Inspector Dunn cautioned the Merrifields in the presence of their solicitor and said, "I am going to arrest you for the wilful murder of Sarah Ann Ricketts."

"I am not guilty," Louisa said.

The summer of 1953 was an eventful one for Blackpool and the UK. In May Blackpool Football Club won its first major trophy, the FA Cup, with local hero Stanley Matthews starring at the age of 38 in the final. A month later, on 2 June, families gathered around tiny black-and-white television sets – those lucky enough to have one – to watch the coronation of Queen Elizabeth II.

On the darker side, the summer headlines also featured two notorious murder trials. On 26 June the serial killer John Christie was sentenced to death for the murders at 10 Rillington Place in London. The other was the trial of Louisa and Alfred Merrifield. This was a period when even regional newspapers had huge readerships. They and the Fleet Street nationals would dispatch battalions of reporters to cover every second of murder trials such as these two. For the trial of Alfred and Louisa, who would eventually be dubbed the "Blackpool Poisoner", the broadsheet pages of the *Manchester Evening News* would devote paragraphs to every glance and throw-away remark during the two-week courtroom showdown.

It began on Monday 20 July at Manchester Assizes before Mr Justice Glyn-Jones. The Merrifields pleaded not guilty. The prosecution was led by Sir Lionel Heald QC, who also happened to be the Attorney General. The first act of the defence was to object to two women being on the jury, an objection that was successful. Both the accused entered the dock flanked by prison officers, Louisa in a grey suit and green hat, Alfred in a brown lounge suit.

One of the first witnesses was Dr Burton Yule, who said he had found Mrs Ricketts dead but had no idea why she had died. He had seen her recently and found her in apparently good health. He had decided not to issue a death certificate, and instead reported the death to the coroner's office. Dr Albert Wood concurred. He had seen Mrs Ricketts the night before her death and found nothing wrong with her.

Poison was, of course, a crucial issue early on. The police had found a shop assistant who eventually identified Alfred Merrifield as the purchaser of the Rodine rat poison. Mavis Atkinson, an "attractive brunette", according to the *Manchester Evening News*, who worked in a chemist's on Victoria Bridge, Manchester, pointed out the man in court "wearing an ear-aid" when asked if she saw one of her customers present. He had been in the shop with a woman. Miss Atkinson said she had been too nervous to identify him when asked to do so on the identity parade (police would testify that she hesitated four times in front of Alfred). Defence counsel Jack di Victor Nahum QC challenged this, suggesting she was now identifying Alfred because she had seen his photograph in the newspapers. Miss Atkinson said she did not read them.

The court heard from several witnesses of Louisa Merrifield's certainty that her employer would soon be dead. Veronica King, who lived on Yorkshire Street, said in evidence that Louisa told her: "I will go and lay the old lady out." This prompted Mrs King to ask if someone had died, to which Louisa said: "She's not dead yet, but she soon will be." This was two days before Sarah Ricketts' death.

Home Office pathologist Dr George Bernard Manning testified that Mrs Ricketts' liver was discoloured, indicating phosphorous poisoning, he suspected. Her heart had probably "given up" after receiving a fatal dose, or doses, during the night before she died on 14 April. The Attorney General would say that phosphorous and bran, both of which were found in Sarah Ricketts, were ingredients in Rodine rat poison. This would have had a vile taste, but Dr Manning said jam, as enjoyed by Mrs Ricketts, would have disguised this.

The defence tried to undermine Dr Manning's conclusion that phosphorous poisoning killed Mrs Ricketts by calling Professor J N Webster, director of the Home Office laboratory in Birmingham. Prof Webster said Manning was "wholly and utterly wrong" and that the pensioner died of necrosis of the liver, caused by poor diet and alcohol. However, he conceded that the phosphorous in her stomach could only have been taken via her mouth.

Even from the vantage point of almost 70 years later, Prof Robert Flanagan found it difficult to say conclusively what the cause of death was. "From what I've read about the case, the victim, Mrs Ricketts, was seen alive at least four days before she was found dead. So, it would appear she was apparently well when seen, and that death had happened quite quickly. Of course, there was debate at the time as to whether it was phosphorus poisoning. One of the senior analysts involved was Professor Webster, who was the Home Office analyst from the Birmingham laboratory. He gave evidence for the defence and was convinced the cause of death was natural causes and necrosis of the liver. Other evidence suggested it was phosphorus poisoning. With it being such a long time ago, it's very difficult to say for certain, in my opinion, what the cause of death was. But obviously, all the circumstantial evidence which surrounded the case pointed the finger at Mrs Merrifield."

Mr Justice Glyn-Jones spent just over four hours summing up. The crux of the case was that the prosecution said Sarah

Ricketts died from phosphorous poisoning, administered via rat poison, while the defence said she died from natural causes, though phosphorous was found in her body. The judge said of Louisa Merrifield, "She is a vulgar and stupid woman, with a dirty mind." This, however, did not mean she was guilty, he added. Of Alfred, the judge said, "He was at times somewhat foolish."

The jury had to decide whether the Merrifields, together or separately, gave Mrs Ricketts poison. Second, did they intend to kill her. Finally, was it the poison that killed her. If the jury answered yes to these questions, they must find the Merrifields guilty, or one of them guilty.

Referring to the bran – the ingredient in Rodine rat poison – that was also discovered in Mrs Ricketts' stomach, the judge made a point that may have helped to undermine the inventiveness of defence counsel Mr Nahum, and therefore Louisa's prospects of being found innocent. The judge said, "It is theoretically possible, Mr Nahum suggested, in all apparent seriousness, that someone may have taken rat poison into the house on his boot. If juries are to be deterred from doing their duty because the ingenuity of counsel can propound some hypotheses, however unlikely, by which the evidence of crime can be explained, then few persons charged with crime would ever be convicted."

The judge advised the jury to rely on their common sense.

The all-male jury deliberated for six hours. The atmosphere was strained and solemn when the court reconvened. The clerk asked the foreman, "In regard to Louisa Merrifield, do you find her guilty or not guilty of murder?"

"Guilty," the foreman replied.

The jury could not reach a verdict on Alfred, who was removed from the dock. Louisa was moved to the centre of the dock, and said, her voice shaking, "I am not guilty, sir."

"You have been convicted on plain evidence of as wicked and cruel a murder as I ever heard tell of," the judge said. The sentence was to be death by hanging.

Justice Glyn-Jones ordered that Alfred be re-tried at Manchester Assizes on 6 October 1953. The Attorney General, however, decided not to pursue the case against him any further. Alfred was released from Strangeways prison on 6 August.

Louisa appealed against her conviction, on grounds including alleged misdirection of the jury by the judge. This was heard at the start of September, but the appeal was rejected, the appeal court judges deciding there was no misdirection and ample evidence for conviction.

How did Alfred escape the same verdict as Louisa? He was described by the defence barrister as a "tragic simpleton", and certainly his repeated protests in court that he could not hear the proceedings probably gave the impression that he was a bumbling old geezer. The judge also called the 71-year-old husband "somewhat foolish".

So, had the all-male jury been taken in by his doddering old man act and judged him less harshly than Louisa? Crime historian Dr Nell Darby did not feel he was the ineffectual buffer he appeared to be in court. She said, "The truth is always more complex than it appears, and Alfred wasn't punished.

But I feel that they lived together, he must have known what she was planning. And I suspect that he was more complicit in what happened than history has remembered. I think that although Louisa was pretty much the driving force behind it and suggested what they should do, it was actually her inability to keep quiet that convicted her. He was better at being docile, being quiet about things. And that's why he got away with it. But I don't think he was as innocent as people believe."

Alfred had actually displayed his astuteness several times. When the solicitor turned up to change Sarah Ricketts' will, Alfred pulled him aside to say he should be included in the will. That's not the behaviour of a "tragic simpleton". When Mrs Ricketts asked him to call on the solicitor because she wanted to alter her will again, probably to cut the Merrifields out of it, Alfred said it was too far for him to go. The next day she was dead.

Although the Manchester shop assistant's identification of him was disputed in court, it could well have been Alfred who bought the rat poison. Most damning, perhaps, was that he was a co-beneficiary of the will, making his motive for killing Mrs Ricketts equal to that of his wife. Louisa clearly did not take him for a fool, telling the woman at the bus stop that Alfred was trying to get Mrs Ricketts to make him sole beneficiary. Whether she really believed that or not, the incident goes to show that she knew Alfred was sharp enough to do her out of her share, given the chance.

Louisa's constant mouthing off to people about how she was "made" and going to inherit the bungalow before Mrs

Ricketts was even dead clearly raised suspicions about her. As did her request to the funeral director to have the body cremated, her repeated warnings to the doctors that the pensioner could die at any moment, and her desperation that they certify Mrs Ricketts as being of sound mind, in case the daughters wanted to contest the will. This is to say nothing of her repeated references to wanting to poison her husband, and her apparent habit of carrying rat poison in her bag.

Her sojourn in prison awaiting the hangman must have been terrifying and bleak, no doubt made worse by knowing that Alfred was free and living in the bungalow he had inherited. Even when he visited her in prison, the old animosity erupted again. The prison governor alerted the Home Office of a shouting match between them on 15 August. In his telegram, the governor, Mr Hair, said, "This afternoon whilst Mr Merrifield was visiting his wife there was a scene during which Mrs Merrifield shouted at her husband, 'Get out of this bloody prison, I never want to see you again.'" It turned out that the *Sunday Dispatch* newspaper was putting Alfred up at a nearby hotel. This suggested his visit to Louisa may have been a bid to get a quote or story out of her for the paper, for which he would no doubt have been paid.

He did, however, write to the new Queen, who had been on the throne for three months that September. In his appeal for clemency for Louisa, he tells "Your most gracious majesty" that his youngest son, Leslie, died serving in the RAF in 1941, and that he himself served with the Royal Engineers in the Great War. He omitted to mention his conviction for abusing an eight-year-old girl. Having assured Queen Elizabeth of his innocence in this case, he asked her to spare Louisa's life.

Louisa's own plea to the Home Secretary, David Maxwell Fyfe, for clemency makes for pitiful reading. The misspellings and errors are a reminder that Louisa left school to work in a mill at the age of 13: "I am Not gilty off this woman Death. there was Nothing in my power that would cause mee to do wrong to this old lady... it is my Duty only, I am to believe by the Power off God, to Plead to you for my life and for mercie..."

She and Alfred had not had easy lives, they abused each other, were crude and broke the law when it suited them. But many working-class people scraped and toiled without resorting to murder. Louisa very probably murdered Sarah Ricketts, helped by her husband, or at least with his acquiescence. But was justice done?

"Should she have been hanged?" asked clinical forensic psychologist Professor Mike Berry. "Legally, yes, because at the time, the judge would put on a black hat and sentence her to death by hanging. That was the normal procedure for a murder. In 1965 hanging was stopped, but in 1953 it was a method of dealing with murderers. The fact that she was a female wouldn't have made any difference."

As for justice, by today's standards Louisa Merrifield paid a brutal price for her callous crime. All requests for a reprieve having failed, she was hanged by executioner Albert Pierrepoint at Strangeways on 18 September. This was the third of three controversial executions Pierrepoint conducted that year, following the hanging of teenager Derek Bentley (condemned for a murder committed by his accomplice) and John Christie (Timothy Evans had already been wrongly hanged for murders committed by him). Louisa Merrifield was one of the last three women to be executed in Britain.

In addition to his duties as hangman, Pierrepoint was the landlord of the Rose and Crown pub near Preston. He found his three headline-grabbing executions that summer turned out to be good for him as celebrity executioner and publican: "The coach park of the Rose and Crown was crowded every night of the summer."

On the gallows, Louisa apparently refused to remove her glasses. Pierrepoint said the execution went well and Louisa had said goodbye to the death-cell officers.

For Alfred, everything was hunky-dory. Three weeks after his wife was hanged, he was interviewed in the *Daily Mirror*. The article had the heading, "This strange man potters on in murder bungalow".

Now residing at 339 Devonshire Road, Alfred was depicted as an "unusual character" who was house-proud of his inheritance. "This is a town that gets used to anything," the feature read. "Freaks are ten-a-penny, and the weird and wonderful happens every day. But even Blackpool cannot get used to the amazing Mr Merrifield."

It reported that Alfred claimed to have made £900 since he got out of prison (around £27,000 today). The reporter tells how he accompanied the old man to the bank with a cheque for £200 (£6,000), received for agreeing to have his effigy added to a seafront waxworks show. He had been offered a further £125 (£3,700) if he sold some of the murder bungalow's furniture.

Instead of being disturbed by living in the home where Mrs Ricketts died, Alfred looked after the place with the "fussiness of a new bride in her first home. The furniture gleams with polish. The chintzes are clean and crisply ironed."

The reporter reveals how Alfred dressed in a gay sports coat and new mackintosh, enjoying the women at the bus stop turning to point him out as he passed. At the seafront waxworks he encouraged the reporter to go in and see the effigy of his wife. Inside, Louisa was standing next to Nazi leaders Adolf Hitler and Joseph Goebbels.

Sarah Ricketts' daughters ended up challenging his position as sole inheritor in her will. It appears he had to settle for a one-sixth share in 1956. He ended up living in a caravan while appearing as an attraction on Blackpool's Golden Mile, billed as the "Murderess's Husband" and regaling gawkers with tales of life with his notorious wife. He died on 24 June 1962 at the age of 80.

Two questions tantalise historians of this case all these decades later.

First, was Louisa Merrifield a serial killer? She bragged to Gertrude Thomas about killing her second husband, Richard Weston: "My last husband was 80, so it didn't take much to polish him off." He had died two months after they wed in 1950, main cause of death being given as "myocardial degeneration", or degeneration of the heart muscle. But Louisa had claimed to have brought this on by giving him a shock.

Richard Weston's son, Daniel, a British Railways official, certainly had his suspicions. After his father's death, Daniel discovered that Mr Weston's bank account had been drained completely of its £1,000 in deposits (equivalent to around £30,000 in 2022). When Daniel asked Louisa, who he only met once on the occasion of his father's funeral, what had happened to Mr Weston's savings, she replied: "He has been very kind to me."

Professor Mike Berry suspects that the poisoning of Sarah Ricketts had been done by an experienced hand. "What I am suggesting is the way it was done was so professional in that she had thought about it," he said. "She knew what she was doing. It wasn't a mistake. We know that she disposed of it [the poison] because when the police went to look in the house, they couldn't find any. So, I'm quite convinced that she would have tried this out in previous situations. She would have known the minimum amount to make somebody ill, and the necessary amount to kill somebody. And it's not as much as people think."

Dr Nell Darby also felt Louisa's marriages raised questions. She said, "There are two ways of seeing Louisa's jumping from man to man. You could say that she was wanting security, especially financial security, and that getting married was her best chance of doing so. But again, it's so quick. She doesn't seem to have that much of an emotional attachment. And you do wonder if there's something darker going on psychologically. Does she see her husband's dying as a way of getting money? I am in two minds, but it all seems a bit too quick to signify just a desire for financial security."

There is, of course, no proof that she murdered a previous husband or husbands, or experimented in the use of poisons on other people. But the fact that she appeared to sometimes carry Rodine rat poison in her bag, and made loose threats about poisoning Alfred and other people, must again inevitably make her appear suspicious.

The second question is about Sarah Ricketts. Because she was the victim of this murder, naturally no one looked closely at her own marital past. But it is a curious fact that Mrs Ricketts was married twice and both her husbands committed suicide in the bungalow. John Green, aged 70, gassed himself at 339 Devonshire Road on 1 November 1942. Just four years later, her second husband, 77-year-old William Ricketts, also gassed himself at that address on 1 August 1946. Ricketts, a retired farmer, left an estate valued at £4,493 (about £133,000 in 2022).

Apart from the coincidence that she had two husbands who committed suicide using the same method in her home, the fact that these deaths were just four years apart seems extraordinary. One husband killed himself in 1942, she remarried in 1944, and then her second, rather well-off husband, committed suicide a couple of years later.

In her statement to police, Louisa said, "Mrs Ricketts told me that she had had two husbands and both gassed themselves in the house. She cried a lot and said it was not her fault."

Nowhere else in any other statements or police reports does Sarah Ricketts come across as a woman who "cried a lot". It is worth bearing in mind that Louisa may be exaggerating here. In this passage she was portraying herself as a devoted companion to Mrs Ricketts, sitting up with her all night. Louisa follows up by lying about Mrs Ricketts' daughters – one being a thief, the other "one of the biggest prostitutes in Blackpool".

What comes across clearly was that Sarah Ricketts could be truculent, wilful, manipulative, even selfish. "I have never met anyone who wanted to live more than she did," said the home help, Lavinia Blezard. The truth is, we just do not know what Mrs Ricketts felt about tragically losing two husbands in quick succession. Perhaps she was emotional when telling Louisa about her husbands, or maybe she was maudlin because she was on a virtually food-free alcohol diet.

It seems apt that a case with more lurid twists than a seafront fairground ride should end with musings on whether one serial killer may have murdered another. But such speculation is as elusive as sea mist.

The facts are that one woman was heartlessly murdered, one executed – and one man with plenty of motive walked free.

Sources

Director David Howard and his team at Monster Films conducted extensive interviews for the *Murder by the Sea* TV series with people who had direct experience of or insights into the cases featured in this volume. Each chapter relies on testimony from the following:

Criminologists and forensic psychologists: Professor Mike Berry, Dr Julian Boon, Dr Nell Darby, Dr David Holmes, Dr Donna Youngs. Victims' relatives and friends: Marelyn Manning, Rhianne Morris, David Tully. Police officers: Paul Bethell, Alyn Chown, Mick Crook, Daniel Cassidy, John Davies, William Glynn, Jeff Harris, Alan Jones, Steve Molyneux, Gordon Shumack, Geoff Sloan, Paul Vacher, Mark Waters, Linda Watkins. Lawyers: Gary McAnulty, Gerard Elias QC. Pathologists: Dr Edmund Tapp, Professor Bernard Knight, Dr Brian Rodgers. Forensic expert: Professor Angela Gallop. Toxicologist: Professor Robert Flanagan. Psychiatric nurse: Chris Kinealy. Plus: Steve Coward, Tim Tate.

OTHER MAJOR SOURCES:
Chapter 1 Stephen Akinmurele
Richard Prothero, Rafal Sikorski, Coastal towns in England and Wales: October 2020, Office for National Statistics, 2020

Chapter 2 Paul Longworth

David Canter, Donna Youngs, Narratives of Criminal Action and Forensic Psychology, Legal and Criminological Psychology, 17, 262–275, 2012

Lindsey Harle, Asphyxia. PathologyOutlines.com website, 2012

Anthony Busuttil, Jason Payne-James, William Smock, Forensic Medicine: Clinical and Pathological Aspects, Greenwich Medical Media, 2003

Chapter 3 John Cooper

Steve Wilkins, Jonathan Hill, The Pembrokeshire Murders, Seven Dials, 2021

Chapter 4 Robert Mochrie

Elizabeth Yardley, David Wilson, Adam Lynes, A Taxonomy of Male British Family Annihilators, 1980–2012, The Howard Journal of Criminal Justice Vol53 No2, May 2014, 117–140

Chapter 5 Pierre Legris

Grahame Allen, Yago Zayed, Homicide Statistics, House of Commons Library Briefing Paper, Number 8224, May 2021

Chapter 7 Penny John and Barry Rogers

Sarah Bloomfield, Classifying Serial Sexual Homicide: Validating Keppel and Walter's (1999) Model, MA thesis, Carleton University, Ottawa, 2006

Chapter 8 Mitchell Quy

James Treadwell, Adam Lynes, 50 Facts Everyone Should Know about Crime & Punishment, Policy Press, 2019

Jill Lobbestael, Vanessa Lea Freund, Humor in Dark Personalities: An Empirical Study on the Link between Four Humor Styles and the Distinct Subfactors of Psychopathy and Narcissism, Frontiers in Psychology, April 2021

Chapter 9 Malcolm Green

National Archives: J 309/171/1, J 309/171/2, J 309/171/3

Chapter 10 Louisa May Merrifield

National Archives: MEPO 2/9536, HO 287/1411, HO 291/230, HO 291/229

DAVID HOWARD is a documentary film maker and founder of the television production company Monster Films. A recipient of the Royal Television Society Award for journalism, his award-winning films include *Interview With A Murderer* (Channel 4) and *Dark Son* (BBC). He is the creator and director of the series *Murder by the Sea*. This is his first book.

ROBIN JAROSSI is a freelance journalist and the author of *The Hunt for the 60s' Ripper*. He is also an on-air contributor to true-crime documentaries on the *BBC* and *CBS Reality*, including *Murder by the Sea*.